"In a time when churches may be searching for quick fixes and programmatic solutions to address congregational stagnancy and decline, we need a reminder of the essence of being the church: a community of people, joined together in the love of God and others. *Never Alone* more than offers such a reminder; it provides both practical and deeply theological resources to create the kind of life-giving community that so many are longing for."

MAGREY R. DEVEGA, senior pastor at Hyde Park United Methodist Church in Tampa, Florida, and author of *Questions Jesus Asked: A Six-Week Study of the Gospels*

"In *Never Alone*, Michael Adam Beck does a fantastic job of helping us reimagine the 'historic' and 'inherited' church as more than a physical place or space. This resource inspires and teaches us how to build and live in community, sharing the good news by daring to be fully ourselves and in authentic relationships with others. A must-read resource of information and inspiration for those seeking to be the church of Jesus Christ in the world today."

OLU BROWN, author of several books, including *Faith: Four Essential Practices*

"In *Never Alone*, Rev. Dr. Michael Adam Beck offers something truly compelling and beautiful. Beck draws from his extensive interdisciplinary knowledge to frame biblical truth *and* provide insightful guidance for confronting the pandemic of loneliness. This book is a must-read for pastors and communities called to Christian ministry in today's world."

REV. LACEYE C. WARNER, PhD, Royce and Jane Reynolds Professor of the Practice of Evangelism and Methodist Studies, associate dean for Wesleyan Engagement, and chair of the Ministerial Division at Duke Divinity School

"The Christian life is life together. Michael Adam Beck knows, lives, and ministers this truth. His book enriches our ability to do the same."

STEVE HARPER, retired professor of spiritual formation and Wesley studies

"This is an invaluable handbook on how to create, sustain, and multiply little pockets of Christ-centered communal life in every neighborhood and village. In fact, Michael Adam Beck believes this is the only way to end the epidemic of loneliness and isolation gripping society today. He makes me believe it is possible. Read this book and you will believe too."

MICHAEL FROST, founding director of the Tinsley Institute at Morling College in Sydney, New South Wales

never alone

MICHAEL ADAM BECK

never alone

SHARING *the* GIFT
of COMMUNITY
in a LONELY WORLD

HERALD
P R E S S

Harrisonburg, Virginia

Herald Press
PO Box 866, Harrisonburg, Virginia 22803
www.HeraldPress.com

Library of Congress Cataloging-in-Publication Data
Names: Beck, Michael Adam, author.
Title: Never alone : sharing the gift of community in a lonely world /
    Michael Adam Beck.
Description: Harrisonburg, Virginia : Herald Press, [2025] | Includes
    bibliographical references.
Identifiers: LCCN 2024038337 (print) | LCCN 2024038338 (ebook) | ISBN
    9781513815183 (paperback) | ISBN 9781513815190 (hardcover) | ISBN
    9781513815206 (ebook)
Subjects: LCSH: Loneliness--Religious aspects--Christianity. |
    Fellowship--Religious aspects--Christianity.
Classification: LCC BV4911 .B43 2025 (print) | LCC BV4911 (ebook) | DDC
    248.4--dc23/eng/20241120
LC record available at https://lccn.loc.gov/2024038337
LC ebook record available at https://lccn.loc.gov/2024038338

Study guides are available for many Herald Press titles at www.HeraldPress.com.

NEVER ALONE
© 2024 by Herald Press, Harrisonburg, Virginia 22803. 800-245-7894. All rights reserved.
Library of Congress Control Number: 2024038337
International Standard Book Number: 978-1-5138-1518-3 (paperback);
    978-1-5138-1519-0 (hardcover); 978-1-5138-1520-6 (ebook)
Printed in United States of America

Unless otherwise noted, scripture quotations are from the Holy Bible, New International
Version®, NIV®. Copyright © 1973, 1978, 1984, 2011 by Biblica, Inc.® Used by permission
of Zondervan. All rights reserved worldwide. www.zondervan.com The "NIV" and "New
International Version" are trademarks registered in the United States Patent and Trademark
Office by Biblica, Inc.®. Scripture quotations marked (BSB) are from the Berean Standard
Bible. Scripture quotations marked (CEB) are from the COMMON ENGLISH BIBLE. Copy-
right © 2011 COMMON ENGLISH BIBLE. All rights reserved. Used by permission. (www
.CommonEnglishBible.com). Scripture quotations marked (KJV) are from the King James
Version. Scripture quotations marked (NRSVue) are from the New Revised Standard Version
Updated Edition. Copyright © 2021 National Council of Churches of Christ in the United
States of America. Used by permission. All rights reserved worldwide.

28 27 26 25 24   10 9 8 7 6 5 4 3 2 1

And remember, I am with you always, to the end of the age.
—JESUS, MATTHEW 28:20 NRSVue

Contents

Foreword

What does it mean to worship a God who is a harmonious micro-community of three? What does it mean to be made in the image of that God? The most accurate pronouns of the triune God should be *they/them*, but in our Western tradition we were formed to focus on the oneness of God rather than the threeness. And thanks to patriarchy embedded in gender-binary language, the oneness has officially been *he/him*.

As I write these words I am sitting at the feet of the Three, rendered in an almost life-size icon of the Trinity that was first painted by Andrei Rublev in the early fifteenth century. This icon occupies the central wall in our communal living room at Spring Forest, a monastic mission community in North Carolina. The Three are arranged in a quietly dynamic circle, seated around a table with a chalice. An open space at the front of the table beckons viewers to join the divine circle. The tender brown faces of the Three radiate humility, vulnerability, and the kind of authority that makes all things new.

The twelve of us who call Spring Forest home see this icon every day, inviting us to the divine table to live in harmony with God, one another, and all living things. The icon challenges systems of power and privilege of our dominant culture that so easily deform our imaginations about what is possible for life together. It calls us to show up every day as a community of love, flawed as we are. The icon reminds us that we are always already seated at that divine table, always already included. We always already belong, even when we do not know it, even when we fail. The icon tells us that we are never alone.

Fostering community is beautiful, complex, messy, hard work, the kind of work that is never done. We make many mistakes. Conflict is inevitable as we jostle against each other with the limited tools we received from our diverse families of origin. Wounds—healed and unhealed—shape our perceptions of ourselves and each other. Life stages affect each of us in our priorities, strengths, and limitations. Spring Forest is a semi-transient community with students and others who come and go. Within this dynamic energy of life together, the icon calls us to center our life around the God who is a community, not ourselves, and for that centering to happen at the table.

In this potent volume, Michael Adam Beck calls us to choose life together rather than life apart. Drawing from Scripture, behavioral sciences, and the wisdom of theologians like Thomas Merton and Henri Nouwen, he invites us to foster communities of love. Writer Margaret Wheatley rightly calls these small, contextual communities "islands of sanity" that we and the world around us desperately need. Indeed, this is what it means to be the church.

May this book open eyes, hearts, and imaginations to what is possible. May it lead us to love and trust more deeply the communal God in whose image we are made. May it remind us that we are never alone.

—Elaine A. Heath, Abbess
The Church at Spring Forest

Going Together

*Loneliness and the feeling of being
unwanted is the most terrible poverty.*
—MOTHER TERESA

My little brother died of a broken heart.

As I sat beside him in the hospital, his chest swelled with air, giving the illusion of breathing. His skin, already sallow, turned an unnatural hue of orange as the dialysis machine was turned off. That device had been circulating fluid into his body twenty-four hours a day for the previous week. The nurse gently rubbed my back, signaling that he was gone.

I clenched his hand, stroking the tear drops tattooed under his eyes, weeping hysterically. Just hours earlier I had signed the papers to take him off life support, one of the hardest decisions of my life.

The fatal diagnosis was an overdose. But the underlying condition was loneliness. It claimed his life at thirty-four years old.

Only two months prior to that day, McKinley was released from a ten-year prison sentence. A decade earlier, in the grips of his drug addiction, he walked into a convenience store and told the cashier to empty the register. At six foot six and 230 pounds of ink-covered flesh, my "little" brother was an imposing figure. He didn't need to use weapons to intimidate people. The cashier obliged, then quickly called 911 when he walked out.

In part because we were from a poor family that couldn't afford legal representation, the judge imposed the maximum sentence on McKinley at twenty-two years old.

Life leading up to that moment was not easy for him. Our mother had been in a lifelong battle with addiction, one that she was losing. McKinley's biological father was an alcoholic and ultimately succumbed to that disease. My biological father was unknown. As kids we ran the streets, broke the law, and struggled to survive. The struggle was paused periodically by trips to the juvenile detention center and later jail.

Upon his release, I was waiting with resources at the ready. At that point, I was in long-term recovery and the pastor of a church that also housed an inpatient faith-based rehabilitation program. But McKinley went right back to his old friends and old ways upon his release from prison. Two months later he was dead.

Yes, technically he overdosed. The people he was shooting up with left him to die when he went down. He lay there, brain-dead, until someone finally found him. By then it was too late. For five days machines kept him alive until I finally made that agonizing decision. It was a week in which time seemed to stand still. All my previous commitments to work and family were paused. There were no parents or responsible adults in our lives to turn to. Besides the consistent support of my loving wife and co-pastor, Jill, it was my little brother and me. Alone.

The encouragement to finally sign the papers came through a vision I received in prayer. I saw McKinley as a little boy, healed, whole, and smiling. A smile I had not seen on his face for many years. Jesus, in a flowing white robe with a face that shone like the sun gently took McKinley's hand and began to lead him down a winding path and into a wonderous garden. McKinley waved as he walked away hand in hand with Christ.

In that moment, the words of Jesus became hyperreal: "I will not leave you as orphans; I will come to you" (John 14:18). McKinley was not alone. Neither was I.

The churches Jill and I lead are also home to a holistic recovery housing program called Open Arms Village (OAV). Men and women live in the same buildings where we hold worship, Bible studies, and committee meetings. On our property are two dedicated clubhouses for twelve-step fellowships. What was once a parsonage (pastor's home) is now a step-up house for Open Arms Village graduates. What was once the pastor's office is now dedicated space for mental health counseling services. My wife and I are on the front lines with people like McKinley every day.

So I had seen people die like this throughout my ministry. I understood the reality of his condition. If I'm honest, up until that moment, I was afraid for McKinley's eternal destiny. That was largely due to the kind of toxic theology that was programmed into me since my earliest experiences with the church. People who don't repent, those who die in their rebellion against God, go to burn in hell—alone—forever.

There were no outward signs in McKinley's life that he had turned to Jesus, and not from lack of poking and prodding from his older brother, the pastor. He died in the depths of his disease. Full of anger at the world, and maybe even a little hateful towards God. But somehow, I felt an overwhelming peace that in that hospital bed, Jesus and McKinley were having a long conversation. I thought of the thief crucified beside Jesus who in the final moments of his life acknowledged Jesus as Lord, to which Jesus responded, "Truly I tell you, today you will be with me in paradise" (Luke 23:43).

A person who had done wrong his entire life, perhaps rightfully executed by the standards of Roman law for his criminal behavior, found grace and an eternity of love. I believe Jesus can see the whole picture of someone's life. The wounds we carry. The traumas that deformed us. I suspect it's not so neat and clean that, unless we repent in our last breaths, the river of God's grace finally runs dry.

I wonder if Isaiah was onto something when he said, "Can a woman forget her nursing child or show no compassion for the child of her womb? Even these might forget, yet I will not forget you. See, I have inscribed you on the palms of my hands" (Isaiah 49:15–16 NRSVue). Though our own mother may abandon us on the side of the road, God will not. McKinley had tattoos all over his body, but God has McKinley's name tattooed on God's hands. Your name is there too. So is mine.

I'm certain McKinley was already in a living hell. A hell of abandonment, isolation, and loneliness. A hell that Jesus already descended into, liberating the captives within (1 Peter 3:18–20). Jesus invited McKinley out of the torment of isolation and into the eternal unity of togetherness.

That day McKinley became an unfortunate statistic. It is a rapidly growing club that no remaining loved ones want to join. Around one hundred thousand people die each year from overdose. It is the largest overdose epidemic in the history of the United States. These are not just numbers in a report, but real people, with real names, and real families who love them. That equates to millions of people who are left to grieve in the wake of their senseless deaths.

But the overdose epidemic is only one feature of a larger phenomenon which includes an increase in mental illness, suicide, and the public health crisis of gun violence, which is now the leading cause of death for children and teens in the United States.[1]

At the other end of the age spectrum was my friend Olive. Olive was a lifelong faithful church member who at ninety-nine could no longer care for herself. Her family moved her into an assisted living facility, but that was the extent of their involvement in her life. As her pastor, I committed to visit Olive as regularly as possible, but I felt as if my presence had little impact.

I watched Olive's body and zest for life fade away. She spent many hours every day in isolation. The nurses did their best to care for her, but with few visitors, little to no communication with her family, and withdrawal from the few communal activities offered by the facility, Olive grew increasingly alone.

Our society is guilty of worshiping at the altar of youthfulness. It flows back to a long series of social transformations that glorified youth, individualism, and self-expression. Following the world wars, and the social revolution of the 1960s, emerging generations rejected social norms including clothing, music, drugs, and sexuality, resulting in the "generation gap." Then began the proliferation of products, procedures, and fitness habits aimed at helping people over the age of thirty achieve the appearance of continued youthfulness. With a cultlike following, all things young are considered to be good, beautiful, and true. In contrast, all things old are irrelevant and antiquated. Ageing is seen as shameful, and people go to great lengths, even as far as pricey cosmetic surgery, to ignore or conceal it.

Unfortunately, the cult of youthfulness is all too ready to discard those ageing beyond their usefulness in a society driven by consumerism. We don't just discard the old device for the new upgrade, we discard people. We warehouse them in facilities, hidden from our shiny, young, Instagram-filtered lives. In so doing we also discard the sage wisdom. We dispose of the voices that our Native American siblings refer to as the "tribal elders." We send them into the oblivion of isolation. And as I will show, this is one of the greatest sins of all.

I believe Olive had more life left in her. I believe her final days should have been more filled with family and friends. People to share her life and wisdom with. Olive died of loneliness.

The epidemic of loneliness

Long before COVID-19 and "social distancing" there was a spiritual sickness destroying more lives than any plague in human history. The virus of loneliness that had been spreading beneath the surface was unmasked during the pandemic. The only cure for this soul sickness is true community, or "social solidarity."

On May 3, 2023, US surgeon general Dr. Vivek Murthy released an advisory titled "Our Epidemic of Loneliness and Isolation." The report details the rise of this epidemic and the significant mental and physical health consequences, including increased risks of heart disease, stroke, dementia, depression, and premature death. Dr. Murthy describes the healing effects of social connection and community and calls for action to address this crisis and emphasizes the importance of building social connections to improve overall well-being.[2]

Although we have never been more connected in human history, we have never been more alone. Isolation is the great soul wound of our time. Perhaps the supercomputers in our pockets that connect us with blazing 5G speed only provide the illusion of connection and a superficial form of relationship.

Pioneering sociologist Manuel Castells was the first to identify the new emerging social structure as the "network society." This society is based less on locality, and is more centered around flows of information and technology. A form of microelectronics-based connectivity allows us to establish distanced contact at the speed of digital light, but it also results in deterritorialization, or the loss of commitment to a place and the bundle of relationships it provides.[3]

In *The Anxious Generation*, Jonathan Haidt explores the impact of digital technology on our youth, documenting the rise in adolescent mental health issues, particularly among Generation Z, due to smartphone use and social media. Haidt suggests we inadvertently ran a mass experiment on our children by giving unrestricted access to the internet and powerfully addictive devices, and by overparenting in terms of not allowing them to socialize through unsupervised outdoor play.[4]

Haight notes a roughly 150 percent increase in depressive episodes among US teens. The increase in mental illness among Generation Z is concentrated in a psychiatric category known as *internalizing disorders*. These are disorders in which one feels strong distress inwardly, including emotions like anxiety, fear, sadness, and hopelessness. Those experiencing these symptoms often withdraw from social engagement.[5]

Robert Putnam, in *Bowling Alone*, through extensive research and analysis documents the erosion of social capital and neighborly good. He explores the diminishing connections within communities and the negative implications for society. In this new social milieu, clubs, civic organizations, and churches are left vacant. Putnam describes this shift as "bowling alone."[6]

It is *not good* for human beings to *bowl alone.*

Surgeon General Murthy suggests that small, meaningful acts of connection can make a big impact, and that faith communities can and must play a role in this. In this primarily secular analysis, religious communities are seen for the benefit of the deep relationships that are formed within them. Amid the increasing trends toward polarization, churches can be one of the few places where people of different perspectives and political views can work together for the common good. The depth of these relationships can lead to increased mental health.

Well-being—physical, mental, spiritual, and social—was the focus of Jesus' ministry. Jesus didn't just love people in a broad sense that lacked particularity. He loved real people, with real names, real gifts, real struggles, and real needs. He loved real families, in real places, in real communities, in a particular time and social reality. In the timeless words of theologian Howard Thurman, Jesus came from a "disinherited" people, with their "backs against the wall."[7] His ministry was one of healing, among those experiencing poverty, oppression, and social isolation.

Jesus stood up in the synagogue at Nazareth and stated that he was the fulfillment of Isaiah's prophecy, "The Spirit of the Lord is upon me, because he hath anointed me to preach the gospel to the poor; he hath sent me to heal the brokenhearted, to preach deliverance to the captives, and recovering of sight to the blind, to set at liberty them that are bruised" (Luke 4:18 KJV). As Jesus went about doing those activities a community sprang up around him called the church. A community where the lonely found connection, where the "brokenhearted were healed."

Matthew 9:36 reports that when Jesus "saw the crowds, he had compassion for them, because they were harassed and helpless, like sheep without a shepherd." The Greek word for compassion, *splanchnizomai*, means to be moved as to one's bowels, hence, to be stirred to the guts. The bowels were thought to be the seat of love and empathy. So Jesus has a gut-wrenching love that inspires him to act.

To describe the overarching health crisis as an "epidemic of loneliness and isolation" is to see the plentiful harvest with the eyes of Jesus, the people "harassed and helpless." Jesus offers an indictment of the shepherds, apparently asleep on the job. The religious leadership of Jesus' day seemed more concerned with upholding ritual codes than tending the relationships between God and neighbor. Perhaps they had collapsed into a state of compassion fatigue, which Jesus called "hardness of heart" (Mark 3:5; 10:5 NRSVue).

How exactly did Jesus' ministry heal the brokenhearted? He did this through the creation of a community. The unbounded kindness of God (Psalm 145:8–9) manifests in Jesus' ministry of compassion. The quality of God's being is expressed through immersion in human vulnerability and suffering, taking on communal expression. The church as the "body of Christ" (1 Corinthians 12:27) in the world is an enfleshment of Christ's own compassion. The continued embodiment of this compassion is a gift. It is in fact the *ultimate gift*.

The role of faith communities

The surgeon general's advisory summarizes the data pointing to the marked decline of religious affiliation since the 1970s and notes its role in increased isolation and loneliness. "Religious or faith-based groups can be a source of regular social contact, serve as a community of support, provide meaning and purpose, create a sense of belonging around shared values and beliefs, and are associated with reduced risk-taking behaviors."[8] Thus, the loss of faith-based groups has contributed to the overall social erosion.

Amid what some have referred to as a traumatized age, clergy quit the ministry in droves. Those in other people-helping professions fare no better, reporting high levels of burnout. Churches across all mainline denominations are declining and thousands close their doors every year.

This is perhaps the saddest news of all, for it is the church alone that has a unique gift that can heal our aching isolation. The church as the body of Christ is eucharistic in nature: it is to be blessed, broken, and given to the world.

The quality of community that is offered in the church cannot be described easily. Perhaps it is better to reappropriate the biblical word—*koinonia* (Philippians 2:1–3). This is a kind of community defined by a depth of interdependence grounded in meaningful relationships. It is a community where we come to know the oneness we already are.

Yet unfortunately most people see the church as a place of harm rather than healing. One in three Americans have experienced religious trauma.[9] The last place they would go to find healing from isolation and pain is the church. Many, like my little brother, try to jam a needle in their arm to escape the aching isolation. We do this in an attempt to fill a hole in the soul that only God can fill. People try to fill that hole with many things: alcohol, shopping, sex, work, social media engagement.

The likelihood that most people will ever walk into the sanctuary of a church building on Sunday morning is slim.

Generationally, more and more people are completely disconnected from a faith community of some kind. Luke reports that an angel announced to a group of shepherds with no significant social standing that the child born in Bethlehem would be "good news that will cause great joy for all people" (Luke 2:10). Even for the lonely, downtrodden, heartbroken, and disinherited. It seems that many see the church today as a community devoid of good news for most people. Rather they see a relic of a past age, with more and more headlines indicating the church is in the bad news business.

What is the "gospel" that Christians claim is a gift worth offering? What historically has it meant across the ages? Can it be proclaimed and embodied in fresh ways in the twenty-first century that bring healing amid an epidemic of loneliness?

The church indeed has one unique gift to offer a lonely and hurting world—communal life in Jesus.

The healing power of togetherness

Many organizations can feed the hungry, clothe the naked, shelter strangers. And Jesus instructs the church to do just that. Yet there is one gift that the church alone can offer. A gift that restores fragmented relationships with God and each other. A gift that re-ligaments us in a new community where loneliness and isolation are healed.

The church has good news to share. A message centered in a Messiah whose name literally means "he who saves" or "he who heals" (Matthew 1:21). The Greek word used to describe how Jesus will "save his people from their sins" is *sozo*, meaning "save." To save is not only about rescue or erasing penalties on a divine score card. It also denotes relief from suffering, healing from disease, or to make well, make whole, and restore to personal and social health.

It's a healing that promises we will never be left alone again. That we will never be forsaken. That isolation is no longer our way of being in the world. And the one who promises this draws us into a community. A community that is both beautiful and broken. Because it is a community where we all share a common peril and are on a shared journey of healing.

This community invites us into a story that has three parts: *goodness*, *aloneness*, and *togetherness*. We are "very good," beautiful, made in the image of God. Human beings in essence are . . . *good*. Made by a good God. We have also been harmed by an original trauma that leaves us all in a wounded condition in some way. In the fallout of that fragmentation, we are left . . . *alone*. But God refuses to leave us there. God comes after us: "Where are you?" We are also being made whole, by God's healing grace, one day at a time. And the journey of grace is one that we take . . . *together*.

In that story we share in a solidarity that makes us a community of equals. The relationships we share restore us to our original intent as beings designed for community and love. In some way, our healing is bound up in these shared relationships. An ever-widening circle of God's inclusive grace, that leaves us alone no more.

Jesus designed his church so that every one of his followers can share that gift. We can all create little pockets of communal life in Jesus in every nook and cranny of life. These communities of gift don't have to happen in church sanctuaries. In fact, they are springing up in dog parks, community centers, substance abuse rehabs, assisted living facilities, and even tattoo parlors. These small expressions are like islands of communal healing in a storm-tossed sea of isolation.

The invitation

This book is an invitation. I'll attempt to expand the meaning of "good news" from the collapsed, individualistic, and mostly post-mortem understanding we have often accepted in the Anglosphere nations.

I do this from primarily two perspectives, the "balcony" and the "dance floor." From the balcony, I am an ecumenical theologian and an applied sociologist. As a seminary professor and researcher, I come alongside students who are the current and future leaders shaping our world. On the dance floor, my wife and I are co-pastors of inherited local congregations that house Open Arms Village, the inpatient recovery program mentioned above.

Every day, we see people who are dying from loneliness, and we see people healed who find real community. My own formal education did not prepare me for ministry in the twenty-first century. In seminary I learned to read Greek and Hebrew, to preach, to order the life of the church, to administer the sacraments, and to provide basic spiritual counseling. I presumed I would be sent to churches where there were people in the pews, yet this is an increasingly inaccurate assumption today. Every pastor must be a missionary now, and every Christian a priest in the "priesthood of all believers."

No one showed me how to be an interventionist: how to develop community partnerships with local therapists, city council leaders, hospital administrators, and directors of residential chemical dependency services. I was not trained to cultivate new faith communities in the ordinary spaces and rhythms of life. "How to develop alternative funding models as the offering plates run dry" was not a course in the curriculum either.

In another sense, no educational institution could fully prepare people for the world today. Few seemed to know that
an epidemic of loneliness, accelerated by a global pandemic,
would be in the cards. Or that most of what we learned in
seminary and clergy residence training was not really that
important—and I say this as a seminary professor myself!
What really mattered would be that we show up, listen well,
and care. The focus of our work would be to connect isolated
people into a community of love and forgiveness that would
heal our lonely lives.

Most of us had not anticipated that the biggest daily challenge would be the loneliness we faced in ourselves and others. That loneliness would be the underlying cause of so many
issues my congregants battle, like heart disease, increased risk
of stroke, obesity, diabetes, dementia, and risk of premature
death. Or that when people snap and resort to firearm violence, it often comes from a place of aching isolation. Or when
they take their own lives.[10]

Then there's addiction. Addiction is a disease of isolation.
I know this firsthand. I used substances to medicate abandonment and loneliness. I sought to mask the insecurities that
flowed from those wounds by using substances to be around
people. For example, while some think of alcohol as merely a
"social lubricant," in the recovery community we call it "liquid courage." For the alcoholic, we rely on alcohol to sustain
the façade of community. In reality, substances only fuel the
enlargement of the false self. For me, as the disease progressed,
I used substances to even get out of bed. Then I discovered
substances were using me all along.

The cycle is vicious: loneliness and addiction, addiction and
loneliness. Community is the cure. But community is hard.
Perhaps the twelve-step recovery "fellowships" understand

the ancient biblical concept of *koinonia* in deeper ways than the average congregation.

Isolation cannot be treated with a pill. Loneliness cannot be removed with surgery. There is only one treatment . . . real community. And real community is not always easy.

I suspect that no matter what your vocation is, no one prepared you to be a healer amid an epidemic of loneliness and isolation either. I wrote this book to try to help. From the base of the once declining congregations we have served, our laity have cultivated dozens of small faith communities called "Fresh Expressions of Church" that gather in the normal rhythms and spaces of daily life. These are communities formed with those who are not currently connected to any church. We do indeed meet in burrito joints, dog parks, running tracks, EV supercharging stations, tattoo parlors, yoga studios, substance abuse rehabs, assisted care facilities, homes, barns, hiking trails, beside bodies of water, and many other locations. I want to share some of our greatest learnings from almost twenty years of this work.

I will suggest a threefold framework for how local congregations and their leaders can reclaim what Michael Moynagh and I have called an "ecclesiology of gift."[11] Ecclesiology refers simply to the study of the church, but this can focus on its relationship to Jesus, its role in salvation, its polity, its discipline, or its structure, essence, and nature. Fundamentally, the essence and nature of the church is a gift . . . blessed, broken, and freely given to all. It is how we can offer communal life in Jesus to a lonely and hurting society. We can be churches who don't wait back huddled together in stained glass sanctuaries, but move out into the world with simple acts of love.

In so doing, fewer people will die from broken hearts, feeling all alone and like there's nowhere to turn. As Surgeon

General Murthy suggests, churches can be communities that disrupt the epidemic of loneliness and isolation. This book is an invitation for how we can do that work together.

It is a practical guide for how every one of us can offer the healing good news. Good news that can be summarized in three words—*Good. Alone. Together.*

Old Testament scholar and theologian Walter Brueggemann describes our common human experience as being "in transit along the flow of orientation, disorientation, and reorientation."[12] *Orientation* refers to being securely oriented in a situation of equilibrium. *Disorientation* captures being painfully disoriented and dislocated. *Reorientation* refers to a surprising move from disorientation into a new orientation that is unlike the old status quo.

Speaking specifically of how the psalms capture these three movements, Brueggemann suggests this is a simple threefold schematic for our life of faith. This pattern synergizes with the three movements of the *Never Alone* framework. Good—orientation. Alone—disorientation. Together—reorientation.

Throughout this book, Thomas Merton, Trappist monk, prolific author, social critic, and poet, will be a primary guide. Henri Nouwen, who was deeply impacted by Merton, called him "one of the most important spiritual writers of the twentieth century."[13] Nouwen is not alone in that assessment.

Okay, let's go deep, let your brain work hard with me for a few paragraphs!

Merton describes the contemplative life as a journey of awakening from the false self, searching for the true self, union with God's self, and communion with the Christ in every person. His profound insights into the "oneness we already are" will help us understand the distinctions between isolation and solitude, guiding us through the communal configurations of the three junctures: *compassionate*, *real*, and *whole*.[14]

Sociologically, the three movements are akin to the three stages in rites of passage described by cultural anthropologist Victor Turner. Turner describes a transition in ritual processes that occurs across human populations, marked by three phases: separation, margin (or *limen*, signifying "threshold" in Latin), and aggregation.

Separation: the first phase signifies detachment of the individual or group from an earlier point in the social structure or the set of cultural conditions. Liminal: during the liminal period, the characteristics of the person become ambiguous, as they "pass through a cultural realm that has few or none of the attributes of the past or coming state." Reaggregation: the final phase is one in which the ritual is consummated, the person or community is once more in a relatively stable state. By virtue of completing the ritual they come into a new "structural" type, a social position in which customary norms and ethical standards are incumbent upon the community.[15]

Theologically these are the three overarching movements of Christian spirituality that I will suggest can be described as *original goodness, original trauma, original unity*.

Original goodness—We were always *good*. This is the movement inward, unmasking the false self, awakening to our belovedness. This can be described as *metanoia*, repentance, spiritual conversion, or a radical turning of heart, mind, and soul. This U-turn journey begins with stopping, realizing we have been traveling in the wrong direction.

Original trauma—We won't always be *alone*. The movement upward into union with Trinity and true self. Eastern Christians have called this *theosis*, a transformative process of becoming one with God. It continues the U-turn of the first movement by now heading in a new direction, towards God and community.

Original unity—We are already *one*. Thomas Merton describes this as the movement outward into communion with neighbor and all life. Historically this has been described as *koinonia*, the quality of shared life together among believers, extended to all. Here we come to the realization that we are not traveling alone at all, we are surrounded by a great cloud of *with*nesses. We are making this journey together.

Okay, now you might be wondering . . . *what does this mean for daily life?* We cannot fully be the good that we already are outside of being known and nurtured in *compassionate community*. We cannot be real alone, but we cannot get real until we are alone in solitude and contemplation. In *real community* we experience divine solidarity. We cannot be made whole, until we are remade together. We are not fully whole until wholeness encompasses everyone, everywhere, and all life. In *whole community*, we experience the unity we already are.

This is the whole gospel, for the whole world.

Later, I will lay out six simple movements called the "loving first journey" as a guide for how teams can travel the three overarching dimensions together. The six movements entail: listening, loving, building community, sharing Jesus (or exploring spiritual practices), forming church, and repeating (or multiplying).

In part I, we will ground the threefold framework in Scripture, tradition, and emerging research. In part II, we will explore practical applications designed to help teams cultivate healing communities that are *compassionate, real, and whole*, in everyday life.

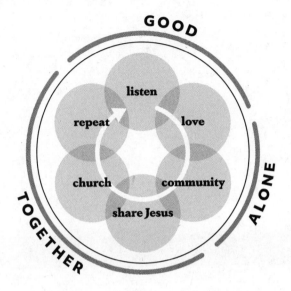

This invitation is not free of danger. Like any worthy adventure there is risk involved. It might challenge long-held assumptions you may hold about Christianity. Once you open yourself to this way of being church, you won't be able to unsee it. So gather a group of people with you. *Go together* on a risky but beautiful journey of sharing the gift of community in a lonely world.

Part I

Love is my true identity. Selflessness is my true self.
Love is my true character. Love is my name.
—THOMAS MERTON

1

Good

God saw all that he had made, and it was very *good. And there was evening, and there was morning—the sixth day.*
—GENESIS 1:31 (EMPHASIS ADDED)

Circle up with me just outside the door of the chemical dependency unit of the inpatient rehabilitation facility in Ocala, Florida. Our team is praying that God will open our awareness to the good things God is doing in the good people inside. After the prayer (and a quick team selfie), we enter, sign in, and go through the pat-down and screening process.

Waiting on the other side of the glass wall are fortyish men and women who currently call this place home. They've been patiently anticipating our arrival (some days are long and there's not much to do inside).

Some of the assembled congregants were court ordered here, others checked in to the detox voluntarily. The gathering is not mandatory but almost all the residents come every week.

"Welcome to Higher Power Hour! My name is _____, I'm a recovering alcoholic and my higher power is Jesus!" the leader proclaims. "We know not everyone who comes here is Christian, that's okay, no matter what spiritual path you are following, or even if you're not really sure about this whole spirituality thing, you are welcome here, and you are loved."

We go around the room and everyone introduces themselves, "Hi, I'm _____, an addict, and my higher power is _____." "Hello, alcoholic _____ and my higher power is_____." Increasingly over the past two years more people fill in that last blank with . . . Jesus. One of our team leaders kicks off a conversation with a Jesus story. This is a short, three-to-five minute impactful telling of something Jesus said or did, placed in conversation with one of the twelve-step principles. The community then shares reflections on the lead, and how it gives meaning to the joys and struggles of their week.

Concluding the service, Chase, our song leader, strums a couple of chords. As soon as her lone voice pierces the air, a choir of voices joins her. The residents know every word. You have not really sung "Reckless Love" until you've sung it together in a rehab with people who are deeply longing for a relationship with God. People whose lives literally depend on that connection with a God who "chases me down, fights 'til I'm found, leaves the ninety-nine."[1]

Jesus was fond of using a series of "You've heard it said . . . but I say . . ." statements. For example, "You have heard that it was said, 'An eye for an eye and a tooth for a tooth.' But I say to you: Do not resist an evildoer," and "You have heard that it was said, 'You shall love your neighbor and hate your enemy.' But I say to you: Love your enemies and pray for those who persecute you" (Matthew 5:38–48 NRSVue). These were controversial statements that reframed people's interpretation of the Scriptures and their understanding of God.

What we are doing in Higher Power Hour is continuing that reframing work of Jesus. At the center of that community is the voice of Christ saying, "You have heard it said, broken, lost, defective, unworthy, but I say to you . . . beloved."

In fact, I believe Jesus' word to the church and world today is this: "You have heard it said, totally depraved, irreparably bad, but I say to you . . . *good*." The world is good. God is good. And *you* are good.

The goodness we already are

In fact, God's first word about humanity is: "very good."

God, a living being of ultimate goodness, is not satisfied to contain goodness in Godself. God shares goodness in the process of creation. God is motivated by love to share Godself, weaving together the particles of our universe in an intricate tapestry of relationships.

God creates in community: "Let us make . . ." (Genesis 1:26). Godself is a community which Christians have historically called Trinity. A God who is One, and a circle of relations, three distinct persons. Merton writes, "He is at once infinite solitude (one nature) and perfect society (Three Persons). One Infinite Love in three subsistent relationships."[2] Creation is a communal effort and a socially constructed environment.

God created the cosmos, a web of good molecules, as an environment for good relationships. Physicists describe the universe as a series of relationships, matter, space, and time, inextricably woven together. God lives in loving relationship with all things and with creation itself. Every molecule is the overflow of God's goodness.

God creates human beings *in relationship* as a triune community, and God creates human beings *for relationship*, with God, one another, and the created universe.

The opening chapters of Genesis describe God's creative process. God imagines the cosmos and then speaks it into existence by word and will. At each stage of creation, the divine

triune community proclaims, "good!" Stars . . . good. Planet
. . . good. Sky, sea, land, and all living things . . . it's *all* good.

The Hebrew word *tov* means "good." *Tov* can mean
beautiful, best, better, bountiful, cheerful, at ease, and fair.
Depending on the context of use it can also denote graciously,
joyfully, kindly, kindness, loving, merry, and most pleasant.

Goodness is baked into every aspect of creation. It infuses
every molecule of the universe. It is the substance from which
all things were made. Think of God baking up a cake that is
the universe; the key ingredient is *goodness*.

When God gets to humanity, we get the first "*very* good!"

In Genesis 2, God gets down in the newly watered mud
of creation and plays around, slapping together mud pie
humans, then breathing into us the breath of life. God takes
the very good earth and stardust, forms very good beings, and
"breathes" (*naphach*) into us the very good breath of life.

When the breath of God enters us, we become *nephesh*
properly, a living breathing creature, a person, a communally
formed self. Genesis 1:27 teaches us "God created humans
in his image, in the image of God he created them; male and
female he created them" (NRSVue). Across the spectrum of
gender and sex we are image bearers, *imago Dei*, formed after
God's own being and likeness.

Created for relationship

Human beings, created in the image of God, and called "very
good," are created to live in loving relationship with God and
one another. Consider how you feel this to be true deep in your
bones. Perhaps you knew it the first time you felt loved and
affirmed by your parents, made a new friend, connected with
your spouse or partner, saw your child's face for the first time.
Reflect on how it materializes in your daily life in a multitude

of simple ways: the smile of a passing stranger, a helping hand in a time of need, the warmth of a hug. Or as Thomas Merton proposes, "The person is constituted by a uniquely subsisting capacity to love—by a radical ability to care for all beings made by God and loved by Him."[3]

God is a relational God. At the final stage of creation, the divine community looks at the work of creation and confers together, "Let *us* make humans in *our* image" (Genesis 1:26 NRSVue, italics mine).

Human beings are created with, in, and for relationship.

As image bearers, we are like a re-presentation of the divine triune community. We reflect the goodness of God and we are given a responsibility over creation. To till and keep, to be fruitful and multiply, to cultivate and care for the creation God has made. We are to live in a loving relationship with creation itself.

Genesis 3:8 tells us, the Lord God regularly walked with humanity in the garden in the cool of the day. Human beings, stamped with the image of God, are companions of God. We share in friendship with God. Can you imagine physically strolling in the garden each day with God as our companion? Having casual conversations with God? So many questions!

This relationship is also a shared power dynamic. There is only one maker: God. We live in a creation that is God's gift to us. Only God can create *ex nihilo* (out of nothing). God alone can start from scratch. We are created beings. We can only work with the existing materials God has provided.

However, God does call us to be co-creators alongside God. One of the first things God did was invite humanity to name each of the living things. Whatever Adam named the creatures became their name (Genesis 2:19–20).

In the Hebrew mindset, naming something was connected to creation. When you named something, you had a kind of ownership over it. Naming is part of the creative process. In inviting humanity to name all living things, God was placing humanity in a place of stewardship over creation.

God establishes humanity in the garden, and then assigns us a vocation, or a calling, that is connected to our very being: "The LORD God took the man and put him in the garden of Eden to till it and keep it" (Genesis 2:15 NRSVue). God places us in creation to *till* and to *keep*. Till—we are to work the land, fertilize it, weed it, and cultivate fruitful things. Keep—we are to care for creation, nurture life, and seek the well-being of all living things.

God gifts us as image bearers, to be his re-presentations on the earth (Genesis 1:27). Meaning we are a re-presentation of God's compassionate care over creation. We are like a mirror that reflects God over creation and reflects creation back to God.

This connects back to our primary vocation in Genesis 1:28:

> God blessed them, and God said to them, "Be fruitful and multiply and fill the earth and subdue it and have domin-ion over the fish of the sea and over the birds of the air and over every living thing that moves upon the earth." (NRSVue)

We are to "be fruitful and multiply," meaning we are to be co-creators with God. We fill the earth with God's image as the *image bearers*. Subduing is not about dominating but rather being the healing presence of God to the harmful tendencies of creation. Dominion is not about asserting our will in a destructive way but overseeing the ongoing flourishing of God's "very good" earth. In short, part of our primary work in the world is to be stewards of creation and co-creators with God in its maintenance and flourishing.

A good species

In *Born to Be Good*, Dacher Keltner, social psychologist at the University of California, Berkeley, suggests that the human species is a compassionate species. He describes our evolutionary journey as *survival of the kindest*. People are often surprised when they learn that Charles Darwin in *The Descent of Man* argued that *sympathy* is our strongest instinct. Darwin surmised, "Sympathy . . . will have been increased through natural selection; for those communities which included the greatest number of the most sympathetic members would flourish best and rear the greatest number of offspring."[4]

Most people associate Darwin and the theory of evolution with the concept of natural selection and the "survival of the fittest." This phrase was invented by his disciple Herbert Spencer, and it is a misportrayal of Darwin's work. Darwin himself argued that our moral capacities are rooted in sympathy. Goodness is a key tendency distinctly evolved in human beings. Kindness, care, and prosocial behaviors are performed with the automatic, well-honed speed of other reflexes. They are in fact stronger than other instincts that move toward self-preservation. Darwin's early formulations of the social instincts of human beings are profoundly grounded in goodness.[5]

What Darwin called "sympathy," Paul Ekman, psychologist and professor emeritus at the University of California, San Francisco, writes, today would be termed empathy, altruism, or compassion.[6] Ekman has been an emotional expression consultant with groups from the CIA to Pixar animation studio, working as a scientific consultant for the animation film series *Inside Out*. Eckman also has a close relationship with the Dalai Lama. Drawing on decades of fieldwork, Ekman explains the evolutionary roots of emotions such as anger, sadness, fear, disgust, and happiness. Following Darwin's lead, he has particularly developed a theory on the nature of empathy and compassion.[7] The ability to feel with and care for one another is a key dimension of our good and compassionate species.

Darwin's *The Expressions of the Emotions in Man and Animals* shaped the modern understanding and study of emotions as evolved and adaptive processes that facilitate communication and connection. Scientific studies demonstrate strong evidence that "compassion and its constituent components, such as empathy, are engendered by body and brain systems shaped by natural selection to facilitate social connection."[8]

Penny Spikins is a professor of the archaeology of human origins at the University of York. Her work explores the prehistoric origins of compassion, arguing that emotional commitments to others seem to have been the basis for in-depth collaboration, which led to evolutionary success. She traces the archaeological record back as far as one and a half million years ago, demonstrating that emotional bonds and motivations to relieve suffering existed in early hominids and distinguished humans from our nearest relatives like chimpanzees and bonobos.

Spikins notes two early examples of care to illustrate this. First is a *Homo ergaster* female (KNM ER 1808), one of the more complete skeletons of the time period found at Kobi Fora in Kenya, which dates back to around 1.6 million years ago. Her bone record demonstrates a severe and fatal case of hypervitaminosis. She would have experienced extreme and immobilizing pain. Yet those around her must have fed her, given her water, and protected her from predators throughout her illness.

Second is the case of the "toothless" hominin from Dmanisi in Georgia, whose skeleton dates back even further to 1.8

million years. While this person had experienced a significant facial trauma leaving them with one tooth, they survived for at least months in this condition as the surrounding bone reabsorbed. Again, they were likely cared for by a community of others.[9]

Cases like this in the fossil record exist among Neanderthals and Cro-Magnons. Early human collaboration must have depended on evolving emotional capacities, to achieve collaborative hunting, food sharing and shared parenting. These tasks required an ability to invest in the well-being of others over one's individual interests. Caring for the vulnerable is one way of demonstrating one's emotional credentials and building trust. No real social cohesion among groups can form without these prosocial behaviors. Our ancestors demonstrate a uniquely human emotional interdependence, based on compassionate responses and emotional commitments to each other, and this played a role in our evolutionary success.[10]

Human beings are indeed innately good. Wired for goodness. We are the compassionate species whose story really is one of "survival of the kindest."

Compassion is not just about helping the vulnerable and marginalized, it's about finding solidarity with others in community. From that solidarity we seek healing together. Our entire body is wired for compassion. We were created for compassion.

Compassion: The infrastructure of relationships

I believe this research compels us to consider that the most appropriate portal into the innate goodness of humanity is found in the phenomenon of compassion. Compassion is foundational to understanding the essence and importance of human community.

Creation itself is an act of compassion. In God's supreme goodness, God wants to share Godself. This is an act of ultimate love.

When we think of compassion, we may assume it starts with suffering. It's the ability to empathize with another, "suffer with" (Latin *compati* "to feel pity," from *com* "with, together"). But our understanding of compassion comes from a fallen perspective. Compassion is not about pity at all.

We were not created to suffer—we were created to love.

As relational beings, created in the image of a relational God, compassion touches on something universal to our nature. The ability to empathize, to think, feel, partner, relate with another being, is at the heart of every relationship. It's the ability to know, to love, to care. Compassion is not merely about helping others experiencing misfortune, it's the capacity for solidarity. Compassion awakens us to the oneness we already are.

Compassion involves an integration of cognitive, affective, and behavioral processes. It includes noticing or sensitivity to another's situation, sense-making related to that situation, feelings of empathetic concern, and then actions aimed at easing or preventing any suffering. The compassion response lights up the amygdala, one of the oldest parts of the human brain. It activates the vagus nerve, a cranial nerve that interfaces with the parasympathetic nervous system which regulates critical body functions such as heart rate, blood pressure, breathing, and digestion.

Let's return to one of the passages that identifies Jesus' compassion. Matthew 9:36 reports that when Jesus "saw the crowds, he had compassion for them because they were harassed and helpless, like sheep without a shepherd" (NRSVue). Again, the Greek word translated compassion, *splanchnizomai*, means to be moved as to one's bowels, hence, to be moved with compassion. So Jesus has a gut-wrenching love that inspires him to act.

This gives us a window into the infrastructure of God's love. Jesus is noticing and attentive to the suffering around him. He is making sense of that suffering: the people are harassed and helpless, the shepherds are asleep on the job. He feels their pain and takes it into himself. His bowels are turned with love, then he acts to alleviate and prevent their further suffering.

Throughout the New Testament, Jesus is moved with *splanchnizomai*, compassion, to heal the sick, feed the hungry, touch the untouchable, and welcome excluded outcasts into the social system. *Splanchnizomai* is one of the central words in some of Jesus' most memorable stories. Consider the parable of the "good Samaritan," a paradoxical tale, being that Samaritans and Hebrews were locked in a bitter sociore-ligious hatred for one another. From the Jewish perspective the Samaritans apparently interbred with their captors and built a new temple on Mt. Gerizim. As a result, they were considered half-breeds, racially and religiously impure.

In the context of an expert in the law asking Jesus a question he most certainly thought he already knew the answer to, Jesus responds with a story. The legal expert asks Jesus what he must do to inherit eternal life. Jesus responds with, "You know the law, what does it say?" He answered, "'Love the Lord your God with all your heart and with all your soul and with all your strength and with all your mind'; and, 'Love your neighbor as yourself'" (Luke 10:25–37). Jesus says, "Bingo, you nailed it, now go and do that and you will have eternal life." But the expert is not satisfied. He wants to justify himself, so he asked Jesus another deeper question, "And who is my neighbor?" (Luke 10:29). Jesus tells the story of a person who is mugged and left for dead on the road to Jericho. This was a path notoriously fraught with dangerous bandits and brigands. A priest, most likely heading back from his responsibilities at the temple, passes by the wounded man. A Levite, someone from the priestly tribe but potentially a layman, also passes by.

The Samaritan, the character who would be the "bad guy" in the story, becomes the anti-hero. He experiences *splanchnizomai*, compassion, and stops to care for the man. He bandages his wounds. Transports him to an innkeeper, and fully funds his healing. The innkeeper nurses the man back to health at the Samaritan's direction. Jesus asks the scribe, "Who was a neighbor to the man?" The expert in the law, apparently unable to use the term Samaritan, says, "The one who had mercy on him" (Luke 10:37). The racially and religiously impure Samaritan, that's right. Jesus says, "Go and do likewise." One could imagine Jesus telling a story about a good liberal, a good libertarian, a good billionaire, or a good atheist. The story would have been shocking to the sensibilities of most Jews. But a more important reading of the story involves how Jesus challenges the accepted socioreligious context with the importance of compassion.

Again, in the story of the prodigal father, compassion is central. Some have called Luke 15 the highpoint of Christian literature. Jesus delivered these parables before an audience that consisted of primarily two groups of people, "tax collectors and sinners," who were drawing near, and "Pharisees and the scribes," who were grumbling about the questionable company Jesus kept. To this mixed crowd Jesus shared three stories that each have a similar structure, theme, and key point:

Something of great value is lost.

What's lost is relentlessly sought after and found.

When what was lost is recovered, there is a party.

In the lost son story, a young man demands his inheritance before his father has even kicked the bucket. This request would be totally inappropriate and massively disrespectful. It would be like saying, "You are dead to me, give me my inheritance now." The father shockingly grants the request. The wayward son quickly squanders his inheritance with riotous living. When a famine strikes, he finds himself feeding pigs, unclean animals, and even willing to eat swine food in the pig trough . . . and "no one gave him anything." (Luke 15:16). This is the ultimate portrait of isolation for a Jew. If ever there was a case study on when to "stone your disobedient child" (Deuteronomy 21:18–21), this is it!

There in the mud of loneliness and desperation the son makes a commitment to go home, willing to repent and be a slave in the father's house. Yet, the father's eyes are on the road, watching, waiting for his son to come up over the hill. While the son is "still a long way off" the father is moved with *splanchnizomai*, compassion, and runs to his son. Showering him with grace, affection, and protection. Restoring him in every way. The three stories are not just about lost things being found. They are about the nature of true holiness, which is inextricably linked with compassion. They are stories about the character and essence of God.

When we see Jesus responding with gut-wrenching compassion, we are glimpsing the anatomy of God's own heart. We are also seeing something that is central to who we are as people created in the image of God.

The cognitive, affective, behavioral dimensions of compassion are merely the physiological hardware of relationships. Its original design is the capacity for empathy. Empathy is a basic prerequisite for relationships. It is the fundamental building block of love.

The original intent of compassion is not about *suffering*, but rather *delight*. To delight in one other. To delight in God. To delight in God delighting in us. This is the true maker's mark in us, and it is the capacity for compassion that has most distinguished the human species.

God delights in the goodness of creation. God delights in us. God delights in us delighting in each other and all life. God gives us the innate ability to delight. This is the foundation of our relational nature.

So then, the first word over humanity is not "totally depraved" or broken beyond repair, but rather "very good." Fearfully and wonderfully made in the image of God.

Social animals

Aristotle, the legendary Greek philosopher, was onto something when he famously stated a version of, "Man is by nature a social animal; an individual who is unsocial naturally and not accidentally is either beneath our notice or more than human. Society is something that precedes the individual."[11] While some of us may be more inclined toward introversion, our social nature is intrinsic to our humanity; in essence we are created by, with, and for relationships.

Social neuroscience is a field of research aimed at understanding biological aspects of social psychological processes and behaviors. As a field, it examines how nervous system (central and peripheral), endocrine system, and immune system are involved in social psychological processes. Thus, social neuroscience seeks to understand underlying mechanisms and consequences of social psychological processes by combining biological and social approaches.[12]

In the 1980s and 1990s, several papers and books began to discuss the "social brain" and how certain brain functions are important for social psychological processes and social behaviors.[13] By the early 1990s social psychologists began to discuss the importance of combining psychological and biological approaches to gain a better understanding of social behavior.[14]

Ultimately these early considerations about the "social brain" inspired researchers from various subfields to begin to use neuroscience approaches to gain insights into social psychological questions and help solve controversies between theories.[15]

While it is considered a relatively new field, the idea that biological responses could be used as a way of measuring social psychological processes, measured by self-reports or overt behavior, stretches back to the third century BCE. A Greek physician named Erasistratus measured the heartbeat of a young man in the presence of his attractive stepmother to conclude that it was not a physical illness but rather love that was causing the young man's ailment.[16]

Neuroscientists can now peer into the brain to see just how wired human beings are for relationships. Using functional magnetic resonance imaging (fMRI) they can in some way glimpse into what parts of the brain activate when viewing familiar individuals in a small social network. Coupled with social network analysis, the imaging shows how the brain activates regions critical for inferring mental states and intentions, as well as regions associated with spatial navigation and psychological distance. In a profound way our brains are wired for connection and relationship.

Often people refer to social neuroscience research regarding these brain mapping aspects, which correlates social psychological processes with certain brain regions. "We have located the part of the brain responsible for _____" is a frequent claim of interpreters of this research. While the kind of one-to-one mapping between psychological function and brain areas is one aspect of social neuroscience, it is very rare and potentially problematic. Increasingly psychological functions are ultimately assigned to entire structures: for example, the anterior cingulate cortex is involved in physical pain, social rejection, cognitive conflict, and more—which provides little benefit for research that tests psychological processes.[17]

For our purposes, one thing that is well established in this field is that the human brain is a social organ. We are a social species, and many of the brain's functions are concerned with *person perception*. Our ability to survive and thrive in this world is largely dependent on our capacity to accurately assess the intentions and behaviors of others. Do they mean us harm? Are they an ally? Can we form an alliance that is mutually beneficial? What is the appropriate form of social interaction? The brain is designed for a massive amount of social perception that often occurs subconsciously.

Community

In the origin of our story is a remarkable portrait of community. Human beings are living together in the garden of creation, in loving relationship with God and one another.

Interdisciplinary research across multiple fields in some sense confirms the biblical account, demonstrating that human beings are social animals. The condition of our social life has a profound impact on our mental and physical well-being. As a species, we need positive, long-term, and committed relationships in order to thrive.

The human species, in terms of Herbet Spencer's evolutionary concept of "survival of the fittest," have a design flaw. We are born into the world with these large brains and small bodies. Our tiny frame cannot support the weight of our own heads as infants. We are helpless, with little chance of survival in adverse circumstances.

In comparison to say, sea turtles, we are not designed to be born ready for the world. Every year Florida beaches are littered with sea turtle eggs. The turtles burst out of their eggs fully independent and begin making the perilous journey towards the ocean. They are often killed by sea gulls, and other predators on the shore and in the ocean. But from the moment they burst out of the egg they are designed for a world where only the fittest survive.

Human beings are designed for compassion. Literally from our first breaths we cannot survive without it. Someone has to love us enough to feed us, clothe us, change us, and protect us. Our only defense mechanisms are tears and volume. Evolutionarily speaking this would be a major design flaw—that is, if we weren't created for love. Compassion is biological, evolutionary, psychological, and sociological. This points to the innate goodness of humanity, not "total depravity." Albeit innate goodness now fragmented and obscured, which we will explore next.

Jesus taught that the eye is the lamp of the body. He referred to some of the religious leaders as "blind guides." They were hard-eyed toward those experiencing pain and subjugation. If the light of compassion dies in us, how deep is that darkness? Have we in some way lost the essence of what it means to be human? This is perhaps having an "eye full of light" (Matthew 6:22). It's the inner light of compassion each one of us is born with.

We cannot thrive outside a context of nurturing love. For those of us who were abandoned or orphaned, it causes wounds to the soul that never fully heal in this life. But in Christ, we can use those wounds to bring healing to others.

Simply put, we are not a species in which *survival of the fittest* is our reality. Rather we are a species who thrives most through love, *survival of the compassionate*. Again, it was the ability for humans to nurture and care for wounded or vulnerable community members that distinguishes us from all other living things. Our ability to love helps us flourish. With this ability comes great responsibility, for the well-being of others and the planet itself.

Compassion is baked into our genetic make-up and wiring. We feel most alive and fulfilled when we are helping and loving others. In fact, we have to work really hard and fight against our own physiological make-up to be jerks. Some of the meanest people I know have experienced significant traumas that have distorted the original goodness within them. In the recovery community we call them EGRs . . . extra grace required. One of the significant challenges of society in the twenty-first century is how it deforms us into patterns of narcissism and consumerism.

Because I'm arguing for the goodness of people, you might be thinking, "This guy is naïve; have you watched the news today?" It's certainly easier to deduce that if humans are good, we sure do a lot of bad. We are constantly flooded with images of violence, death, sickness, political extremism, and natural disasters. While we are a species wired for *survival of the kindest*, we inhabit a social system that operates on *survival of the fittest*. It's true, I am very familiar with the human capacity for evil. But if we look hard enough, even among all those realities, we will find those Fred Rogers called "the helpers." Good people, doing good things, in the fallout of the bad.

My belief in human goodness comes from a commitment to regularly be face-to-face with the bad. Every week, at Higher Power Hour sitting in that substance abuse rehab, women and men share horrible stories of the bad side of human nature. Some who were abandoned and abused as children, turned to drugs, alcohol, and sex to cope with the wounds. They freely share about their own darker moments, confessing violence, sex work, stealing from family members, knowingly spreading STDs, and giving away their children to the disease.

Yet so many of these stories are turning into songs of hope and healing, as they seek to enlarge their spiritual lives. They describe going on a journey of liminality and disorientation. They celebrate how they have shared a common peril and have now been re-ligamented in a new *koinonia* community. They describe this community as a "family" in which God is like a loving mother and father. Now they are learning to love themselves and others. They are being re-formed for community. By God's healing grace, they are returning to their original design.

Most of the members of this faith community are unlikely to set foot in a traditional worship service on a Sunday morning. So we are being church with them where they live. This is a community that doesn't need to be reminded of how terrible we were. We are already well aware of this. We are healing together from the guilt and shame of our past. It's also not a community where fear of hell in the afterlife is in any way a motivator for our ongoing spiritual development. We have already been to the hell of isolation and loneliness, got the T-shirt. We are a community who has in some sense been rescued from a living hell of a life, and for some our higher power is Jesus.

Our journey of healing begins by deconstructing harmful images of God and self, coming to terms, many for the first time, with the reality that there is a God who loves us. A God who is affirming us. A God who sees the goodness we don't always see in ourselves. The first step of our faith journey is embracing our belovedness. Unlearning the mask of the false self. Learning self-compassion. Receiving the unlimited and free gift of God's grace. Going back to the garden.

We all have a garden origin story. No matter who we are, we begin life utterly dependent for survival on the quality of our relationships with our primary caregivers. Our survival as a species hinges on the capacity for social living. From the dawn of human history, we have formed small groups of community for survival and flourishing.

Our well-being is largely determined by the duration and quality of our relationships. One aspect of our very goodness is our formation for community.

We are ultimately good. Created by a good God. To dwell in a bundle of good relationships.

Original goodness—the good we always were. This is the first of three movements in this "good news for all people."

So where did all the bad come from? Why is it so pronounced? In Genesis 2:18, we get the first "not good" in our story. It is *not good* for "humans to be alone." Human beings created for relationships are not made to live in isolation. Now we turn to the second movement in our journey . . . the aloneness we weren't made for; the alone we won't always be.

2

Alone

The Lord God said, "It is not good for the man to be alone."
—GENESIS 2:18

Good, good, very good . . . *not good*!
At the tail end of Genesis 2 we hear the first "not good" in the creation story. It is not good that humanity should be *alone*. As relational beings we are created for relationship. Isolation, loneliness, lack of community, is *not good*.

In this garden paradise there is only one restriction: Don't eat of a single tree, for if we eat of that tree, we "will surely die." In Genesis 3, a strange newcomer to the story arrives, a talking serpent. The serpent beguiles humanity into doing that very thing we should not do, manipulating us into thinking there is something more that God is withholding. It's not enough to be made in the "image of God" but we want to be "like God."

This strange character also exploits us in our state of child-like innocence. The talking serpent slightly twists the truth, and asks a misleading question, "Did God really say?" The seed is planted in our sinless minds that God is withholding something, that there is a relational distance between ourselves and God. God doesn't want us to eat the fruit because our eyes will be opened in a new way.

In one sense, this is an act of abuse. The serpent, who later we will discover is "the father of lies" (John 8:44), goes about like a "roaring lion" seeking the wounded and vulnerable to devour (1 Peter 5:8). Manipulation, grooming, and the resulting wounding can be considered a form of exploitation that leads to "the fall."

Humanity caves to this temptation. We certainly have a part to play, but we didn't get there on our own. And yet, we cannot build a theology around the idea "the devil made me do it." The whole witness of Scripture, and thousands of years of Judeo-Christian tradition, won't let us get there. As Michael Fishbane, scholar of Judaism and rabbinic literature, so concisely states, "The serpent is *with* us in the world, *without* us in the world, and *within* us in the world."[1]

As the prophet Jeremiah reminds us, "The heart is deceitful above all things and beyond cure. Who can understand it?" (Jeremiah 17:9). It's not merely some fallen angel who is deceitful above all things, it's something inside us. The Bible asks us to hold together in creative tension that we are made "very good" in the image of God, and that something in us has gone horribly wrong.

Being created for relationship is our greatest strength but it also makes us vulnerable. Not all relationships are good relationships, and some can cause great harm. Nevertheless, one of the first sin impulses is *isolation*.

Male and female flee from God and themselves, hiding naked in the garden. Our guilt drives us away from each other and from God. We have done a bad thing and isolation seems to be the appropriate response, breaking away from the intimacy that led to our wounding. We also experience a new phenomenon . . . shame. Initially, Adam and Eve were both naked, and they felt no shame (Genesis 2:25). After we have tasted of the fruit of "good and evil" suddenly "the eyes of both of them were opened, and they realized they were naked; so they sewed fig leaves together and made coverings for themselves" (Genesis 3:7). Now, we feel devalued, like we were a mistake, not just that we did a bad thing, but that we are bad creatures, who need to hide from God. Shame drives us toward a state of isolation; isolation breeds within us the emotional condition of loneliness.

The implications of this action are like a stone being thrown in a pond, the impact causes ripples in the water that stretch out across the entire cosmos. Every aspect of creation and everything is affected. All that is "very good" is also now wounded and fragmented. This is our *original trauma*, the aloneness we weren't made for and won't always be. All of this occurs at the level of relationships. Isolation is the fallout of sin.

Isolation

The Old Testament vocabulary for sin is extensive, numbering over forty words. The large number of terms indicates the concept has central importance in the narrative of Scripture. Some have argued that essentially the Bible is about how God deals with and restores a fallen humanity from sin.

In general, sin is about disloyalty and disobedience, which is located in breaching a *harmonious relationship* with God, ourselves, and nature. The first word the Bible uses for sin occurs not in the garden of Eden, but when Cain slays his brother Abel. This first occurrence emanates from the lips of God "If you do well, will you not be accepted? And if you do not do well, sin is lurking at the door; its desire is for you, but

you must master it" (Genesis 4:7 NRSVue). We will return to
this story momentarily.

The word "sin" used here is *chatta'ah*: an offense, sometimes a habitual behavior, and its penalty. It is the most frequent word for sin in the Old Testament (occurring in different
derivatives nearly six hundred times), and it denotes "missing
the mark." Metaphorically speaking, think of when an archer
is aiming at a bulls-eye and misses the target.

More specifically, it signifies falling short of the expectations inherent in certain relationships. Other Old Testament
words for sin, like *pasha*, specifically describe actions that rupture social solidarity and shatter relational harmony (e.g., to
break away, trespass, apostatize, quarrel, offend, rebel, revolt,
transgress). Such behaviors tear the social fabric of communal relations.

The key theme of the biblical material is that sin extends
to all human beings and has contaminated every possible relationship. Sin fragments our relationship with God. It affects
our relationships within the family and our neighbors. It is the
opposite of shalom—peace, safety, and well-being—which is
God's intent for creation. It disrupts the possibility of peace
within the family and society at large.

Sin distorts and disrupts the patterns of nature, our relationship with the land, with plant life, with animal life, and
with the world itself. Historically the word *depraved* has been
used to communicate this state. Not that every person or relationship is totally depraved, but that sin has the potential to
rupture every relationship.

The Old Testament has a very specific way of speaking
about guilt. The word *asham* occurs more than forty times
in the Pentateuch (first five books of the Bible) and describes
being guilty and by implication to be punished or perish. It

describes less a matter of conscience, and more the state of being for one who has acted wrongfully. A person is in a state of guilt between the act of sinning and the punishment. A helpful parallel could be closer to the modern conception of being cursed. Biblically, guilt is like a curse or stain of sin.

Sinful actions bring pain to God. The effects of human sin harm God, the offended person, the sinner, human community, and nature. Through sin we are driven from the presence of God in the garden. Cain is driven out as a wanderer. This theme of migration, wandering in the wilderness of sin, and exile, are prominent throughout the Old Testament. Through sin, we are distanced from God and from others.

Isolation is all at once an act of sin, the consequence of sin, and an ongoing state for the sinner. When we harm others, we fragment and sever relationships. We enter a state of isolation through our sin. We live in a state of isolation, separated from God and one another. The ultimate separation in the Pentateuch is the state of death itself.

Let's move toward interpreting the human condition theologically, while applying a sociological analysis. Imagine that we are innocent children, and a trusted family friend shows up, manipulates us, and abuses us in some way. Our innocence is stolen. Our relationships are fragmented. In our pain, we might act out and cause harm to others. Pain causes us to devalue relationships. It usually starts by devaluing ourselves. Hurt people hurt people, as we say in the recovery community.

This is the universal human condition. The trauma that we carry from this abuse is like a virus. Wesleyans describe this as "in-being sin," which refers to some distortion in our original nature that bends us toward the *not good*. Every person and every living thing is born infected with it. It's embedded in our cells in a latent way. We need healing from this infection.

Isolation is the virus that leads to death, and death itself is the ultimate loneliness. It is into this state that we, innately good beings, are born. Historically theologians have called this "original sin."

Our first defense mechanism is self-preservation. We hide. We conceal. We play the blame game. "The woman made me do it!" says Adam. "The devil made me do it!" says Eve. However, the damage is done. Sin enters the picture, which emerges as a fragmenting of the relationship with God and each other.

Where are you?

Fortunately, in the very next scene, we find God coming to the garden with the gentle call, "Where are you?"

Where we are in that moment is naked, afraid, and aware of our nakedness and afraidness. This virus has caused a transformation in our consciousness. Our eyes are opened in a new way. One aspect of this new condition is the two-headed monster of guilt and shame. Guilt, in the social psychology sense, is like a God-given alarm system for the soul. It alerts us to the reality that we have done something wrong and need to make amends. Shame is toxic and never good, a side effect of the virus. It has to do with a warped self-image. Guilt says, "I made a mistake and need to make it right." Whereas shame says, "I am a mistake and have no worth."

"Where are you?" This is God's response. Is it really that God doesn't know where we are? Is it possible to hide from God?

I love playing hide and seek with my grandchildren. Several of them have not learned object permanence in their development. Once an item disappears, to their little minds the item no longer exists. So when they close or cover their eyes with their hands, they do not exist. Because they can't see me, they assume I can't see them. They are hiding in plain sight with their eyes covered, crouched down in the middle of the room. Of course, as good parents and grandparents we play along. Who enjoys a game of peek-a-boo more? Adults or our little ones?

It's unlikely that God doesn't know where we are. Like little toddlers we are hiding in plain sight. The question is a proximity question, "Where are you in relation to me?" It's a love question, "What have you done that has led you to hide, conceal, and isolate from me?"

One of the consequences of our actions is death. Human beings, made to live in eternal loving union with God, must now "surely die." Adam will suffer through fruitless work, toiling in land that has itself become cursed. The very goodness baked into creation is now polluted with sin. The good mud and stardust from which we are made now has a level of toxicity. Eve will now experience the pain of childbirth, creating community through blood and agony. The social relationships are also now corrupted; from coequals, helpmates, partners, made equally in the image of God, now there seems to be a fallen hierarchy we will later call patriarchy (Genesis 3:14–19).

An innate consequence of this fracturing occurs primarily at a relational level between the serpent and humanity, "enmity between you and the woman, and between your offspring and hers" (Genesis 3:15). Conflict, struggle, relational disharmony seems to be a pervading feature of a new sin-warped cosmos.

Death is not only a consequence for humanity, but now animals become food, and garments (Genesis 3:21). Reminder, since killing and eating creatures is a result of the fall, we all begin our story as vegetarians or fruitarians! All animal and plant life are also affected. Predatory species emerge. The divine community confers and decides to expel humanity from the garden, lest they exist eternally in some kind of undead, fallen state. We lose access to the tree of life, for now. The good world has gone wrong (Genesis 3:21–24).

Unfortunately, our story doesn't get much better from there. In the very first generation, we have the first case of premeditated murder. Cain, jealous of the Lord's approval of his brother Abel's more heartfelt sacrifice, rises and kills his own brother in an empty field. The God who calls out "Where are you?" is in conversation with Cain throughout this scene. Apparently while our sin has earned us dismissal from the garden it has not stopped God from pursuing ongoing relationship with us. God warns Cain that sin crouches, waiting to master him, but "you must master it" (Genesis 4:7 NRSVue).

While the blood of Abel is still warm on the ground, God asks Cain, "Where is your brother Abel?" The chilling response to this question has haunted humanity ever since, "I do not know; am I my brother's keeper?" (Genesis 4:9 NRSVue). Judging by the Lord's reaction, the answer is a resounding "Yes," we are all indeed our sibling's keeper. We are created to live in loving relationship together. Stewarding these relationships is the essence of what it means to be human. Perhaps murder is the ultimate act of sin because it is the irreversible act of not only depriving someone of life but depriving another person of the benefit of living relationships.

Cain is driven out into his own kind of isolation, to be a wanderer and a fugitive. Cain, recognizing the significance of this curse cries, "My punishment is greater than I can bear! Today you have driven me away from the soil, and I shall be hidden from your face; I shall be a fugitive and a wanderer on the earth, and anyone who meets me may kill me" (Genesis 4:13–14 NRSVue). Cain shall be disconnected from the presence of the Lord, disconnected from others, and targeted with the same kind of violence he inflicted upon Abel. Even so, God vows to protect Cain from murder. While the prevalence of sin consistently takes the main stage, it is persistently outshined by the prevalence of God's loyal love and grace. A God who continually calls out "Where are you?" amid our isolation.

Alone together:
Counterfeit community and tools of loneliness

Sadly, by Genesis 6, things have gone from bad to worse. A strange interbreeding has taken place, which some speculate was the union of fallen angels and humans resulting in the mysterious "Nephilim." Again, further evil is attributed to some kind of outward interference.

"Not good" takes on epic proportions: "The LORD saw that the wickedness of humans was great in the earth and that every inclination of the thoughts of their hearts was only evil continually. And the LORD was sorry that he had made humans on the earth, and it grieved him to his heart" (Genesis 6:5–7 NRSVue). God feels the pain of this situation. God grieves. God's heart hurts. The only way to heal the mess is a kind of reset, a flood that might provide a fresh start. For there is at least one righteous family worthy of the effort, Noah.

An often-understated aspect of sin and one we will return to later is humanity's relationship to creativity and the technologies we generate. When Cain goes "out from the LORD's presence" he settles in "the land of Nod, east of Eden." He marries and has children there. Where the people of Nod originated has perplexed biblical scholars for centuries. But it seems Cain and family turn to technology as a way to live in isolation from God. They build a city where they create the first "stringed instruments and pipes" and where they "forged all kinds of tools out of bronze and iron" (Genesis 4:16–22). Their technology has become a kind of tool to normalize loneliness.

Perhaps this is the first attempt for humanity to live "alone together." This phrase originated from MIT sociologist Sherry Turkle, whose work we will return to later. In *Alone Together*, Turkle explores how technology shapes our relationships and self-perception and argues that despite feeling more connected, we're actually becoming more isolated due to digital interactions.[2]

That's what's happening out there in Nod. Noah, on the other hand, uses technology for good purposes. He builds an ark that can house his family and pairings of every living animal in the world. The structure becomes a holding space for human community, and a tool to sustain relationship with God as the waters above and below burst forth to re-create the world.

Shortly after the flood, humans are back at it again, settling on a plain in Shinar, utilizing a new technology, brick-baking and mortar, to construct a tower. They say, "Come, let us build ourselves a city, with a tower that reaches to the heavens, so that we may make a name for ourselves; otherwise we will be scattered over the face of the whole earth" (Genesis 11:4). Apparently, this new tech will create a quick fix counterfeit form of community, to stay together and not be "scattered over the face of the earth."

God is not pleased. The Lord comes down to inspect and sees the mischief we are up to. God is concerned that in utilizing this technology, and speaking the same language, we will amplify our creativity in fallen ways to live apart from loving union with God. The divine community confers, "Come, let us go down and confuse their language so they will not understand each other" (Genesis 11:5–7).

God responds with another form of migration and exile, "So the LORD scattered them from there over all the earth, and they stopped building the city. That is why it was called Babel—because there the LORD confused the language of the whole world. From there the LORD scattered them over the face of the whole earth" (Genesis 11:8–9). Perhaps we see here that not all forms of community are *good* community. Twisted versions of communal life seek to exclude God from the center. It is possible that the technologies we are using today create a shallow and inauthentic Babel-like form of community. *Un*real community.

And yet, as devastating as this narrative may seem thus far, a God who comes to the garden with the compassionate call "Where are you?" is good news for a people who often ache with isolation. A God who doesn't withdraw divine presence from us when we fail and fall. A God who even when we have done the most heinous thing imaginable to our own brother, still shows a degree of grace and unfailing love. A God who will start all over for a single good family. A God who won't let us live apart in a dystopian, shallow, counterfeit form of community that utilizes our technologies to live apart from God.

This is a God of love. This is a God committed to authentic community. Real community. And the entire Bible is basically the story of a compassionate God calling out "Where are you?" ever since. A God who delights. A God who cares. And a God who hears our cries and feels our suffering (Exodus 6:5–8). A God who never gives up. A God who will never leave us . . . *alone*.

Loneliness, isolation, and solitude

Have you ever scrolled through your social media feeds, seeing the faces of "friends and followers," and thought to yourself, "I am so alone." Here we are, connected with people from across the span of years and geographies of our lives, and yet we can't shake the sense that something is missing. As hyperconnected as we are, we feel the emotional pain of loneliness. You are not alone in that feeling.

So if loneliness and isolation are an epidemic today, what really are they? And is it always "not good" for us to be alone? What about the spiritual practice of solitude? Surgeon General Vivek Murthy has written a helpful book, *Together: The Healing Power of Human Connection in a Sometimes Lonely World*, to help us understand.

While closely related concepts, loneliness and isolation are not the same thing. Loneliness is a subjective feeling that we are lacking social connection. Loneliness is an emotional experience. Isolation is the objective physical state of being alone and disconnected from others. The state of isolation can lead to loneliness, as we will often feel lonely when we are isolated from the community. However, one can be in a room full of people and still be experiencing loneliness. And yet, being isolated doesn't always translate to the emotional experience of loneliness.

Biologically speaking, we are wired for connection and relationship. It is an essential aspect of our humanity. Murthy writes, "Quite simply, human relationship is as essential to our well-being as food and water. Just as hunger and thirst are our body's ways of telling us we need to eat and drink, loneliness is the natural signal that reminds us when we need to connect with other people."[3]

When our stomach growls, we know we need to get something to eat. When our throat feels parched, it's a signal to get something to drink. When we feel tired and sluggish, it can be due to lack of enough quality sleep. When we feel lonely, it's a signal that we need connection and companionship.

Dr. Murthy summarizes research to describe three dimensions of loneliness. Each dimension reflects particular types of relationships that are missing.

1. Intimate, or emotional, loneliness is the longing for a close confidant or intimate partner, someone with whom we share a deep mutual bond of affection and trust.
2. Relational, or social, loneliness is the yearning for quality friendships and social companionship and support.
3. Collective loneliness is the hunger for a network or community of people who share your sense of purpose and interest.

The lack of relationships in any of these dimensions can make us lonely.[4]

So then, loneliness is a near universal human condition. We all experience it at times, just like when we get off balance with proper diet, hydration, or sleep. Our social well-being is connected to sustaining quality relationships in these various dimensions. Yet when we feel lonely, we often retreat into further isolation, rather than toward connection and community.

Furthermore, we can turn to unhealthy behaviors to cope with the emotional state of loneliness. As discussed earlier, people use drugs, alcohol, food, or sex to numb the emotional pain of loneliness. Combined with the stigma associated with these choices, this creates a cascade of consequences that not only affect our personal health but societal well-being. We not only hurt ourselves, but we often hurt others, and this tears at the very social fabric of our communities.

One coping mechanism for loneliness is the supercomputer we carry around in our pockets. We can turn to those devices in unhealthy ways. I have found myself at times "doomscrolling," mindlessly swiping the screen for hours, only to come out of a hole later feeling like an entire day disappeared. While games, watching videos, and other online activities may distract us temporarily from the ache of loneliness, it returns with a vengeance when our battery dies. Social media may provide the illusion of connectivity and make us feel we are part of a collective, but often the superficial nature of those relationships merely masks our isolation.

We can begin to feel shame associated with our loneliness, and for the subsequent coping behaviors. Murthy describes loneliness as a harmful cycle: "Shame and fear thus conspire to turn loneliness into a self-perpetuating condition, triggering self-doubt, which in turn lowers self-esteem and discourages us from reaching out for help."[5]

We feel shame that we are lonely. We embrace harmful self-perceptions: I'm not a person worthy of friendship, I am not enough, I am unlikeable, no one really cares if I live or die. That spiral of declining self-worth leads us further toward isolation and ever deeper into the emotional pit of loneliness.

Solitude on the other hand is something entirely different. Here we must make an important distinction. Is it always "not good" to be alone? What do we do with the pattern of advance and retreat in the life of Jesus himself? Jesus often retreated away to the solitary place (*eremos*, or wilderness) to heal and rest. This is a consistent rhythm in Jesus' life: periods of high activity and then solitude. Amid all the activity and crowds pressing in, Jesus withdraws to the solitary space. There in the quiet place, in prayerful communion with the Father, Jesus is refreshed. He doesn't allow himself to be led by the whim of crowds or clamor of notoriety. This is Jesus' normal rhythm, periods of intense, socially impactful ministry, and restful withdrawal into the solitary space. It is a rhythm of advance and retreat.

Thus, we need to distinguish between isolation and solitude. Isolation is a long-term physical distance from other people, while solitude is usually short-term. Isolation results from our own unhealthy behaviors, and it is often forced on us by circumstances. We isolate ourselves when we retreat into our own fear and pain. Solitude is a practice we choose as part of a spiritual lifestyle.

Solitude is usually a spiritual practice whereas isolation is a sin instinct. We actively seek solitude for ongoing spiritual development.

Later we will explore the three stages of the journey of spiritual transformation that Thomas Merton describes: awakening from the false self, searching for the true self, and union with God's self. This journey inward and upward into union with Trinity and true self requires solitude. However, Merton's idea of the union we experience with God through the solitude of contemplation is not about withdrawal from the world. He writes, "The only justification for a life of deliberate solitude is the conviction that it will help you love not only God but also other men."[6] Discovering our true self leads us into deeper levels of union with everyone, everywhere.

Merton believes that all of us are shadowed by an illusory person, a "false self." "To say I was born in sin is to say I came into the world with a false self. I was born in a mask."[7] Becoming real to ourselves and to God is actually the only pathway to become real to others. It reconnects us to the original unity.

In short, solitude is not separation, and contemplation is not perfect until it is shared. It is a way of being in the world. "The more we are alone, the more we are together; and the more we are in a true society, the true society of charity, not of cities and crowds, the more we are alone with Him."[8] We seek solitude to reconnect with God, our neighbor, and ourselves. We seek isolation when the world becomes unsafe, and we want to hide. In fact, sometimes forced isolation can either break us or move us into solitude.

Solitary confinement

Across history, human beings have concocted some terrible ways to punish and kill each other. Reaching back to the eighteenth century BCE, Babylonians burned people alive for certain offenses in accordance with the law code of Hammurabi. Ancient Egyptians made a spectacle of some executions, by dressing the offender in ceremonial garb for public torture and death. The Romans announced their dominance through crucifixion, nailing people to a wooden crossbeam to bleed out slowly and suffocate under the weight of their own body. In ancient Japan, certain offenses were punished with being boiled alive. During the fifteenth century CE, Vlad III, Prince of Wallachia, is credited as the first notable figure to prefer the ancient practice of impaling as a favored method of execution, hence his endearing nickname, "Vlad the Impaler."

The modern world has seen mass genocide, concentration camps, and atomic bombs. Execution is still carried out today through electric chairs, beheadings, gas chambers, and lethal injection.

But what if I told you one of the most inhumane forms of punishment is perfectly legal and is happening to hundreds of thousands of people in the United States and abroad, right now, today?

The practice to which I refer is solitary confinement. The United States incarcerates more people per capita than any other developed nation. We also have one of the largest percentages of people kept in solitary confinement. A 2023 report found that more than 122 thousand incarcerated men, women, and children were held daily in some form of isolated confinement in US prisons and jails.[9]

If it is "not good for humanity to be alone," if we are truly created for relationships, and sin is ultimately isolation, solitary confinement is a living hell on earth. It is one of the most cruel and calculated forms of torture that exists in the twenty-first century. As Merton reminds us, "The man who locks himself up in private with his own selfishness has put himself into a position where the evil within him will either possess him like a devil or drive him out of his head."[10]

I can speak to this not only from a theoretical perspective but from my own experience. As a street kid, I grew up in juvenile detention facilities and state programs. In my BC (Before Christ) life I was involved in selling and using drugs and the whole ecosystem of crime associated with that activity.

My first charge as a fourteen-year-old juvenile was possession of a large quantity of marijuana with intent to sell. I was arrested, stripped naked, deloused, given an orange jumpsuit, and given a mat to sleep on on the hallway floor of an overcrowded juvenile detention center. Today, I could simply file for a business license with the state, set up shop, and legally distribute medical marijuana to those in need. I was a real pioneer. Seeking to help the ill attain their important medicine. I was just born about twenty years too early.

This exposes the injustice of an economic system driven by profit and not morals, and a corrupt justice system that is driven by the bottom line. Nevertheless, in juvie I learned how to be a real criminal. I learned to fight better. I learned what other criminals my age were doing better. I made new connections with those criminals, and we formed alliances.

Years later, after the accumulation of more felonies, I found myself lying on the floor of a solitary confinement cell in the Marion County Jail. By that time, I was a full-blown drug kingpin, working with a network of shady doctors who over-prescribed opioid narcotics so I could conveniently distribute them in the streets. I also used these opiates. Lots of them. I took hundreds of milligrams of OxyContin every day for years.

So after I was arrested, I began to experience significant withdrawal. That included vomiting, diarrhea, muscle pains, cramps, hallucinations, and many other symptoms. As general population is often a less than ideal place to go through withdrawals, in order to get myself out I started a fight. After resisting the guards physically and receiving a beating in kind, I was arrested again and taken to solitary confinement. I found myself in the jail inside the jail.

I have seen some horrible places in my life, but nothing comes close to the darkness of the solitary confinement pod. We were locked down in a small room twenty-four hours a day. There was only a small shaft of light through an obstructed window and a chow slot where food trays were placed three times a day. With no clocks or calendars, we counted the days through the three meals.

Some of the most hardened criminals are broken by time and isolation. Suicides are regular occurrences in "segregation housing" as inmates find a way to hang themselves with their bedsheets or slit their wrists with a shaving razor. The condition of those who were mentally ill was aggravated by the isolation; they banged on the iron doors and ranted gibberish night and day. Inmates intentionally injured themselves, banging their heads on the walls attempting to get moved to medical.

Some of my neighbors were more creative; they stored up feces and urine, waiting for the opportunity to sling it on the guards. A CERT (correctional emergency response team) squad would come in and physically beat those inmates severely. They would get stitched up and sent right back, with more time to do. And in some cases, inmates die from guard-inflicted violence.

Solitary confinement is hell on earth. Minutes seem like hours. There is no stimulation. No one to turn to. Only the disorted voice of the false self, whispering lies. For human beings wired for compassion, there is no place to give or receive care. It is a compassionless place of torture. Many people do not survive that kind of incarceration and those who do are traumatized for the rest of their lives.

My saving grace was a mysterious prison guard, who walked into the unit and placed a Bible in my chow slot. I never saw her again and I suspect she was an angel of some kind. For forty-five days I went through withdrawal and read that Bible in the sliver of window light. In my case, the isolation turned into communion. I encountered the Risen Jesus in that solitary confinement cell. I experienced his presence, as a being of pure compassion. I physically felt him wrap me in light like a hug. I relived every horrible thing I had ever done, and pleaded for forgiveness for the harm I had caused to so many. Amid the ache of guilt and shame, I saw the whole picture of my life through his eyes, and heard him continually affirm, "Beloved." There I began to confront my false self, turning inward and upward to my true self in Christ.

It was incarcerated in the belly of the jail where, completely confined, I experienced freedom for the first time. I encountered the God named Immanuel, "God with us." Sadly, solitary confinement destroys so many others. A cage of isolation, where we are truly left alone, is in some sense a denial of a core aspect of our relational nature. It is a dehumanization that destroys image-bearing persons of sacred worth and infinite value. Yes, even criminals, born "very good" into corrupt and discriminatory systems, who are often merely reenacting the cycle of unhealed trauma that they experienced in their own lives.

Not every person has to go to a solitary confinement cell to realize the healing power of solitude. Most people don't have to commit felonies to begin the movement from false self to true self. And yet every person has experienced or is in some way experiencing a solitary confinement cell in their own way. It is the universal condition of the wound of the *original trauma*. We have been separated, fragmented from ourselves and others. We have experienced exile or migration, or have fled from the presence of God and one another. We all stand equally in need of healing. And that healing can ultimately only be found through communal life in Jesus.

3

Together

I will not leave you as orphans; I will come to you.
—JOHN 14:18

For he himself has said, "I will
never leave you or forsake you."
—HEBREWS 13:5 NRSVue

The spiritual life has been referred to as a marathon not a sprint, a long obedience in the right direction. There is an African proverb that is helpful here: "If you want to go fast, go alone. If you want to go far, *go together.*"

As human beings made in the image of God, created by, with, and for community, it is through togetherness that we find true fulfillment and healing.

Sociologists affirm the deeply communal nature of the human species. They can also measure how different cultures value human relationships. Consider that sociologist Robin Williams (1965) famously identified the core values of US society: achievement and success, individualism, hard work, efficiency and practicality, material comfort, and freedom, to name a few.[1]

These are values of an individualistic culture. Indeed, Surgeon General Murthy writes, "The values that dominate modern culture elevate the narrative of rugged individualist and the pursuit of self-determination. They tell us that we alone shape our destiny. Could these values be contributing to the undertow of loneliness I was witnessing?"[2]

Individualistic culture contrasts with collectivistic culture. Consider the Bantu anthropological framework of *ubuntu*. The Zulu concept of ubuntu highlights the interdependency of humanity. All individuals are woven together in a single interconnected organism, so that even a small act of love impacts the entire world.

Ubuntu emphasizes that a person is a person through other persons. One person's humanity is inextricably linked in a bundle of life with all others. We are relationally determined beings. The ecosystem of relationships we share make us who we are in deep ways that are often imperceptible to us. The concept of being an isolated individual, lone decider of our story, is in some ways false and deceptive. It perhaps traces back to that first age-old temptation. It's not enough to be made in the image of God, as a relational being, interdependent on others. Communal in the very essence of our being. We want to be "like God."

Amid individualistic cultures the church is a countercultural phenomenon. The church asks us to lay aside our personal preferences for the betterment of the community. It calls us to do life together even when we disagree.

The Bible originated from a collectivistic culture. It describes One God who is a collective of three distinct Persons. Or perhaps a connective, the Godhead community, diverse singularity. The Bible tells a collective story, and a connective story. It is the story of one peculiar people, but it is also the story of all people. The Hebrew people are socially collectivistic in their worldview and perspective.

Good, alone, together—A journey begins

An obscure God reaches out to a good couple, Abram and Sarai. This God calls them to leave behind the urban center they have called home, Ur of the Chaldeans. They are to pack up their family and leave the bundle of relationships they have known. They are to go alone, wandering into the unknown on a journey of orientation, disorientation, and reorientation. The destination of this journey will end in the ultimate form of togetherness.

This family, called out from the civilization they knew to go on a journey toward a promised land, would become the ancestral parents of a people in whom "all the families" of the mud and stardust would be blessed (Genesis 12:1–3 NRSVue). A vision of all the diverse tribes of humanity living in a blessed communion has been called the "Abrahamic promise."

The journey will be filled with many faults and failures, twists and turns. Although God has promised to make Abram and Sarai into a "great nation" they are well beyond child-bearing age and remain childless. Even so, God gives Abram a new name: no longer will his name be called Abram, "father of many," but his name will be Abraham, "father of multitudes." God says, "For I have made you a father of many nations. I will make you very fruitful; I will make nations of you, and kings will come from you. I will establish my covenant as an everlasting covenant between me and you and your descendants after you for the generations to come, to be your God and the God of your descendants after you" (Genesis 17:5–9).

Way past retirement age, Abraham feels compelled to sacrifice his one and only son, conceived by Sarah. With his son

Isaac bound to the altar, knife in the air, Abraham hears an angel's voice, halting the blade, and suddenly a sacrificial ram appears in the thicket. While other gods of the ancient world might require child sacrifice, not this God. Not YHWH. If this feels like it rubs against your own faith tradition, keep reading, because I'll dish about this in part II.

For Abraham's willing obedience to sacrifice the child he's been waiting for his whole life, the promise becomes even clearer. "I will surely bless you and make your descendants as numerous as the stars in the sky and as the sand on the seashore. Your descendants will take possession of the cities of their enemies, and through your offspring all nations on earth will be blessed, because you have obeyed me" (Genesis 22:17–18).

Sarah and Abraham will possess the whole land of Canaan, where they now reside as foreigners, and it will be an everlasting possession to them and their descendants. And YHWH will be their God.

The one requirement that God asks of Abraham is this: "As for you, you must keep my covenant, you and your descendants after you for the generations to come" (Genesis 17:5–9).

Somehow in the fallout of sin, the isolation, the fragmenting of relationship between God and humanity, God's plan to put it all back together is through this one family. One family that will become multitudes. One peculiar family through whom all the tribes and families of the earth will be brought back together. A peculiar people who live in *covenant* with God.

A covenant of togetherness

Generations later the descendants of Abraham find themselves enslaved in Egypt. This strange God is no unmoved mover, no God who is disconnected from the triumphs and struggles of life. This is a God of relationship. A covenant-keeping God.

In a primarily secular society, we assume a frame of life in which we dismiss the possibility of a God who can break in and affect our reality. When we experience harm and marginalization in our own lives it's easy to assume that God doesn't care. That if there is a God, that God is far away and removed from our daily life and emotions. But the God we encounter in Scripture pushes against these secular assumptions.

YHWH says, "I have indeed seen the misery of my people in Egypt. I have heard them crying out because of their slave drivers, and I am concerned about their suffering. So I have come down to rescue them from the hand of the Egyptians and to bring them up out of that land into a good and spacious land, a land flowing with milk and honey" (Exodus 3:7–9). This peculiar God indeed feels the suffering of the people. God is sensitive to their plight, assessing the causes and conditions, then is moved with compassion to act and liberate.

God choses to do this through an unlikely candidate. God calls an Egyptian fugitive, formerly a prince, named Moses to square off with the most powerful person in the ancient world. Moses, a murderer of an Egyptian taskmaster, must go before Pharoah and demand the release of the people. After quite a showdown that involves numerous plagues, as if through a sequence of disasters creation itself seems to unravel, Pharoah finally releases the people.

Thus begins the journey through the wilderness and towards a promised land. It is along the journey that God establishes this promised covenant. In the Old Testament, a covenant is a legally binding obligation, establishing the basis of a relationship, conditions for that relationship, promises and conditions of the relationship and consequences if those conditions were unmet. The covenant can be thought of as graceful boundaries through which God's peculiar people are to live in relationship with God and one another.

Some helpful imagery might be thinking of the covenant in terms of a marriage relationship. When two people come together and commit to a lifelong union, we often recite some version of these vows, "In the name of God . . . to have and to hold from this day forward, for better, for worse, for richer, for poorer . . . to live together in holy marriage . . . and forsaking all others, be faithful . . . till death do us part."

I never thought of my marriage to Jill as a legally binding contract. I made a commitment to the woman I love. I committed to live within relational boundaries of our marriage covenant. Choosing to live those vows every day until we die. Choosing to love each other even after the honeymoon was over. Yet there is a legal element to a marriage covenant.

At the core of the Old Testament covenant is the Ten Commandments—the Decalogue. These boundaries are about how to live in loving relationship with God and one another. It's as if God is saying to Israel, I'm choosing you to be my precious spouse. Here's what I expect:

> I am the LORD your God, who brought you out of Egypt, out of the land of slavery.
>
> You shall have no other gods before me.
>
> You shall not make for yourself an image in the form of anything in heaven above or on the earth beneath or in the waters below. You shall not bow down to them or worship them; for I, the LORD your God, am a jealous God, punishing the children for the sin of the parents to the third and fourth generation of those who hate me, but showing love to a thousand generations of those who love me and keep my commandments.

You shall not misuse the name of the LORD your God, for the LORD will not hold anyone guiltless who misuses his name.

Remember the Sabbath day by keeping it holy. Six days you shall labor and do all your work, but the seventh day is a sabbath to the LORD your God. On it you shall not do any work, neither you, nor your son or daughter, nor your male or female servant, nor your animals, nor any foreigner residing in your towns. For in six days the LORD made the heavens and the earth, the sea, and all that is in them, but he rested on the seventh day. Therefore the LORD blessed the Sabbath day and made it holy.

Honor your father and your mother, so that you may live long in the land the LORD your God is giving you.

You shall not murder.

You shall not commit adultery.

You shall not steal.

You shall not give false testimony against your neighbor.

You shall not covet your neighbor's house. You shall not covet your neighbor's wife, or his male or female servant, his ox or donkey, or anything that belongs to your neighbor. (Exodus 20:1–17)

The Ten Commandments are all about relationships. The first four are about honoring our relationship with God. The next six are all about honoring our relationship with our neighbor. I am massively oversimplifying the Old Testament concept of the covenant here. There are actually a series of "covenants" and 613 Levitical restrictions that come later.

However, it is noteworthy that Jesus essentially summarizes "the greatest commandment in the Law" as two categories of love: "'Love the Lord your God with all your heart and with all your soul and with all your mind.' This is the first and greatest commandment. And the second is like it: 'Love your neighbor as yourself.' All the Law and the Prophets hang on these two commandments" (Matthew 22:36–40).

The purpose of the covenant is missional. Through Israel, all the families of the earth will be blessed. God reveals that if they keep the covenant, they shall be a "treasured possession out of all the peoples" and "a priestly kingdom and a holy nation" (Exodus 19:5–6 NRSVue). In serving in this priestly capacity, Israel will mediate God to the world, and the world to God. As the people live together in loving relationship with God and one another, it will be a witness to all humanity. It will be the way God blesses all the families of the earth (Genesis 12:3).

Unfortunately, the people demonstrate their inability to uphold these relational expectations. Rebelling again and again. Being unfaithful in the marriage. The story becomes a seesaw of good and bad kings, holy and corrupt priests, moments of hope followed by utter betrayal and despair. God sends prophets to turn the people back to the covenant of love, but they are mistreated, ignored, and even murdered.

The psalmists and prophets begin to speak of a coming messiah king who will inaugurate a peaceable kingdom. A God-Man savior who will set everything right. Who will put back the pieces of the fragmented relationships between God, humanity, and the creation.

God, speaking through Jeremiah, states, "The days are surely coming, says the LORD, when I will make a new covenant with the house of Israel and the house of Judah. It will not be like the covenant that I made with their ancestors when I took them by the hand to bring them out of the land of Egypt—a covenant that they broke, though I was their husband, says the LORD" (Jeremiah 31:31–33 NRSVue). This passage takes up the very imagery of a violated marriage. Rather than God giving up, even amid our unfaithfulness, God offers a "new covenant."

A decisive change will take place where the covenant is not words inscribed on a tablet, or sacred scrolls, but cut into the human heart muscle itself, "But this is the covenant that I will make with the house of Israel after those days, says the LORD: I will put my law within them, and I will write it on their hearts, and I will be their God, and they shall be my people" (Jeremiah 31:33 NRSVue).

Ezekiel refers to this procedure as a heart transplant, "I will give them one heart and put a new spirit within them; I will remove the heart of stone from their flesh and give them a heart of flesh" (Ezekiel 11:19 NRSVue).

One thing often overlooked by Western interpreters is that these are *communal* images. This is what God will do with a *community* of people. The community of people God will use to bring about the restoration of all communities, of all tribes, of all families. Good news of great joy for *all people*.

And then, in the fullness of time.

Jesus—Expanding the guest list

"I feel like there's something not quite right about a Jesus wrapped in an American flag and MAGA hat, or a Jesus dressed in drag, but it seems like the churches I have visited are only offering those two options," says Jessica, sitting crosslegged on a yoga mat. We have gathered for Yoga Church. A fresh expression that shares in a brief "Jesus story," a short telling from the life and teaching of Jesus, followed by a dialogue and yoga flow.

What Jessica is describing are some of the distortions of cultural Christianity. Of course, there is no such thing as a noncultural Christianity; Jesus did after all incarnate himself in a particular culture, and there is no version of Christianity that is not a cultural expression. In another sense, there are "cultural Christianities" that are Christian in name only. For example, Christian nationalism is a distorted version of the faith. A Jesus surrounded by armed patriots, calling for insurrection, willing to shed blood in the name of the Prince of Peace. Drag queen Jesus is also a distortion. Both are parodies of Jesus, a Jesus we created in our own image.

Generation Z folks like Jessica are sniffing out the whiff of falseness here, and rejecting those distortions. They want the real thing. And the troubling truth about the real Jesus is that he welcomes both the person wearing the MAGA hat *and* the person in drag equally to his table.

Jesus is the fulfillment of an ancient promise of togetherness that stretched back all the way to the obscure wandering family of Abraham and Sarah. The fulfillment of God's "Where are you?" call to put humanity back together.

Similar to the earlier situation back in Egypt, in Jesus' day the Jewish people were one minority who lived under the subjugation of the Roman Empire. They were an oppressed people with little political or military power. Jesus was not part of the dominant or majority culture, but rather he belonged to a group of people who existed at the bottom of a social, political, and economic hierarchy. Jews were an ethnoreligious minority, one of many religious groups among the conquered subjects of Rome.

In Jesus' time, to be a Hebrew was to be part of a tribal family that traced its ancestry back to Father Abraham. There was a strong in-group and out-group dynamic. A Gentile, meaning someone not of the genetic lineage of Abraham, would have to go through a ritual conversion process which included circumcision to become a Jew.

Jesus was in every way a faithful adherent to that group. He participated in the sacred rituals, rites, and pilgrimages appropriate for a Jewish male. While there seems to be a missional thrust to the Abrahamic promise of Genesis 12 that all nations "would be blessed" through Israel, the religious leadership of Jesus' day seems to have been reading it in mostly an exclusive way.

It appears that in Jesus' more heated exchanges with the religious leaders of his community, some adherents had taken on a posture of what we could call today exclusivity. The two dominant religious groups, Pharisees and Sadducees, seemed to have certain ideas around how their ancestry placed them in an elite and superior class.

Jesus seemed to challenge the air of superiority that accompanied the temple system. His statement that the temple would be destroyed and that "not one stone will be left here upon another" (Matthew 24:2 NRSVue) would have been shocking and offensive to many Jews.

Alongside the temple, synagogues spanned the Roman Empire. *Synagogue* is a term synonymous with both a gathering of people and a place where they gathered. Jesus had controversial encounters with both the temple priests and the synagogue leaders. His well-noted temple tantrum in which he flipped over the tables of the money changers and accused them of turning it into "a den of robbers" (Matthew 21:13) seems to be a social and theological critique of their activity.

Immediately following the disruption, Matthew tells us, "The blind and the lame came to him at the temple, and he healed them" (Matthew 21:14). Jesus' ministry with the disinherited draws the ire of both the "chief priests and the teachers of the law" who when they saw the wonderful things he did and the children shouting in the temple courts, "Hosanna to the Son of David," became indignant (Matthew 21:15).

Additionally, Jesus had several unpleasant encounters with the Pharisees (and others) in the synagogues which resulted in his near execution. For example, in Nazareth when he identified himself with the messiah in Isaiah, the people sought to throw him off a cliff (Luke 4:16–31). When he challenged the Pharisees' traditions about the Sabbath they began to plot how to execute him (Matthew 12:1–14; Mark 2:23–3:6; Luke 6:1–11). When Jesus placed himself above the Pharisees' level of authority they plotted his killing (John 5:1–18). And when Jesus told the chief priests and Pharisees that the kingdom of God would be taken from them and given to another *ethnos*—a tribe, nation, or people group—they looked for a way to arrest him (Matthew 21:33–46; Mark 12:1–12; Luke 20:9–19).

It seems the leading response of these religious leaders in these heated encounters with Jesus was to default to their ethnic and religious superiority. For instance, a consistent defense of the religious leaders seemed to be that they could claim superiority based on ancestry, "Abraham is our father" (Matthew 3:9; John 8:39). In John 8 when religious leaders pull the ethnic superiority card "Abraham is our father," they go on to accuse Jesus of being a "Samaritan and demon-possessed" (John 8:48). Again, Samaritans were a group they labeled as racially and religiously impure, and inferior. Jesus indicates that their ancestry claim might be valid, but it's irrelevant, for they are in the presence of one who was before Abraham. They respond expediently by picking up stones to execute him (John 8:58–59).

Indeed, it seems the most revolutionary claim in the life and teaching of Jesus was that these religious ideas of superiority and exclusion were being turned upside down. This was an aspect of the kingdom he came to proclaim, in which he was anointed to "bring good news to the poor . . . proclaim release to the captives and recovery of sight to the blind, to set free those who are oppressed" (Luke 4:18 NRSVue). A kingdom where, in order to enter, one must repent, rethink, turn around and move the other direction (Mark 1:15).

This was a core component of the "good news of great joy for all the people" (Luke 2:10–11 NRSVue). This was the "mystery that has been hidden throughout the ages and generations but has now been revealed to his saints" (Colossians 1:26 NRSVue). It's quite clear that one aspect of the mystery involves "to make known how great among the gentiles are the riches of the glory of this mystery, which is Christ in you, the hope of glory" (Colossians 1:27 NRSVue).

So when Jesus tells the religious leaders, "The kingdom of God will be taken away from you and given to a people that produces its fruits" (Matthew 21:43 NRSVue), he is indeed turning all their claims of superiority inside out: the Gentiles, the *ethnos*, are being invited into the kingdom as equals beside them.

Jesus seemed to have a bad habit of reaching beyond the in-group, healing, blessing, and even calling Gentiles to be his followers. Suffice it to say Jesus was constantly breaking the social barriers and reaching out to people who were different. We see him constantly pushing the boundaries and expanding the concept of who was "neighbor." Jesus reaches out to the cursed ones with withered limbs (Mark 3), the untouchable lepers (Luke 17:11–19). Jesus reaches out to sinners, tax collectors (Luke 15), and sex workers (Luke 7:36–50; John 8:2–11). In fact, Jesus demonstrates that the scope of "neighbor" is massive in scale; it includes people from every race, tribe, and nation (Revelation 7:9).

Jesus' ministry was one of radical inclusion and an ever-expanding guest list to the heavenly banquet. The new covenant involves all people everywhere. Jesus heals the fragmentation of those relationships from the fallout of the original trauma, making it finally and fully possible for all the families of the earth to live in a state of blessed communion and togetherness.

The God who calls "Where are you?," the God who from the very beginning is trying to put that fragmented relationship back together, comes after us. Not just through liberation from bondage in the exodus, but life-giving laws that give graceful boundaries for life in the covenant, and prophets who offer course corrections along the journey to wholeness as we "fail forward."

Ultimately, God heals this breach of relationship by coming to us in the person of Jesus Christ. He refuses to be God without us, so he becomes Immanuel, "God with us" (Matthew 1:23). Jesus is the embodiment of God's garden call, "Where are you?" He's the God who comes to find us and rescue us from our fragmented state. He heals us of the disease, restoring us fully to "very goodness."

This is partly accomplished through the cross. The unbounded mercy of God manifests in Jesus' ministry of compassion and finds ultimate expression on Golgotha, the "hill of the skull" where Jesus was crucified. The quality of God's being is expressed through immersion in human vulnerability and suffering, expressed most fully in the passion of Christ. Thus, in Jesus, we encounter the traumatized God.

God's nature is the self-emptying (kenotic), other-oriented, and sacrificial love fully displayed in the crucifixion. The cross is the *way* of Jesus.

While all of Jesus' life, incarnation, and presence with us now make this healing available to us, it is through the cross that the virus of aloneness is cured. Jesus physically isolates the virus of sin in his own body on the cross, taking it into himself and destroying it. "He carried in his own body on the cross the sins we committed. He did this so that we might live in righteousness, having nothing to do with sin. By his wounds you were healed" (1 Peter 2:24 CEB).

The "rulers and authorities" gather collectively at the cross and are "disarmed" and triumphed over in a public spectacle (Colossians 2:15 NRSVue). All the forces of moral and natural evil—imperial evil, religious evil, demonic evil—converge literally in an earthquake in one place, in one moment in time (Matthew 27:51). There, concentrated in the pain-wracked body of Jesus himself, with the virus of loneliness isolated in his own flesh (2 Corinthians 5:21), he takes on our shame in himself (Hebrews 12:2), and destroys its power through his own sacrificial death (1 Corinthians 15:55–56).

Through the resurrection, ascension, and sending of the Spirit, every Christian, in union with Christ, becomes a microcosm of Jesus, a cell in the larger body. We become the antivirus, spreading reconciliation throughout the whole fragmented cosmos (2 Corinthians 5:18), until Jesus returns to bring the new creation in all its fullness (Matthew 24:30; Revelation 21–22).

It's a relationship with this living Jesus (union) through which our healing comes. A relationship that is available to all people through a broken and beautiful community called the church. Sadly, many forms of church today are known for their radical exclusivity, which becomes even more problematic when we consider the implications of Pentecost.

Pentecost: Togetheversity

Ultimately, God has fulfilled the Abrahamic promise through Jesus Christ. In the first Pentecost God literally creates a new social arrangement and a new humanity (Acts 2). The author of Acts explains,

> When the day of Pentecost came, they were *all together in one place*. Suddenly a sound like the blowing of a violent wind came from heaven and filled the whole house where they were sitting. They saw what seemed to be tongues of fire that separated and came to rest on each of them. *All of them were filled with the Holy Spirit* and began to speak in other tongues as the Spirit enabled them.
>
> Now there were staying in Jerusalem God-fearing Jews *from every nation under heaven*. When they heard this sound, a crowd came together in bewilderment, because each one heard *their own language* being spoken. Utterly amazed, they asked: "Aren't all these who are speaking Galileans? Then how is it that each of us hears them in our *native language*? Parthians, Medes and Elamites; residents of Mesopotamia, Judea and Cappadocia, Pontus and Asia, Phrygia and Pamphylia, Egypt and the parts of Libya near Cyrene; visitors from Rome (both Jews and converts to Judaism); Cretans and Arabs—we hear them *declaring the wonders of God in our own tongues*!" Amazed and perplexed, they asked one another, "What does this mean?" (Acts 2:1–12, emphasis mine)

What does this mean indeed? The outpouring of the Spirit at Pentecost is how God puts back the pieces of Babel in which we tried to use technology to live in counterfeit community apart from God. Peter, empowered by the Spirit, points to its significance as being fulfilled by the prophet Joel:

No, this is what was spoken through the prophet Joel:

> "In the last days it will be, God declares,
> that I will pour out my Spirit upon all flesh,
>   and your sons and your daughters shall prophesy,
> and your young men shall see visions,
>   and your old men shall dream dreams.
> Even upon my slaves, both men and women,
>   in those days I will pour out my Spirit,
>   and they shall prophesy.
> And I will show portents in the heaven above
>   and signs on the earth below,
>   blood, and fire, and smoky mist.
> The sun shall be turned to darkness
>   and the moon to blood,
>   before the coming of the Lord's great and
>   glorious day.
> Then everyone who calls on the name of the Lord
> shall be saved." (Acts 2:16–21 NRSVue)

God is pouring out the Spirit "upon all flesh," not just a select few anointed ones, but everybody. Part of this new reality includes the fact that women and men "shall prophesy," and the normal constraints of age will be transformed, young people will have visionary foresight and wisdom, and older people will not lose the capacity to dream. Further, the economic and social caste systems are now upturned, slaves are no longer at the bottom of some invisible pyramid but are equally empowered. The barriers of patriarchy and sexism have also been reversed, "both men and women" have received this outpouring, and they can supernaturally function in the gifts of the Spirit.

These are all reversals of the curse that came into being through the fallout of the original trauma.

What we see in that first outpouring of the Spirit is *togetherness*. The disciples are united in prayer, *together* in one place. We also see *diversity*. Representatives from every tribe and tongue under heaven together in one place.

Togetheversity. There is unity, oneness, *koinonia*. There is also diversity, distinctness, including every *ethnos*. A plurality of people and languages, hearing each other, singing the same story.

In the book of Revelation, we get to peer through the curtain into the new creation just behind the veil. In that coming-soon future we see:

"After this I looked, and there was a great multitude that no one could count, from every nation, from all tribes and peoples and languages, standing before the throne and before the Lamb, robed in white, with palm branches in their hands. They cried out in a loud voice, saying, 'Salvation belongs to our God who is seated on the throne and to the Lamb!'" (Revelation 7:9-10 NRSVue).

In that vision, we see Jesus' earthly prayer finally fully answered, "Thy kingdom come, thy will be done on earth as it is in heaven." We see the final fulfillment of the Abrahamic promise and the conclusion of the outpouring of the Spirit at Pentecost.

"In Christ"

The giving of the Holy Spirit creates a universe-altering shift in the categories of human existence. It opens a fresh possibility of restored relationship with God. God literally comes to make his home *in us*. Historically, we have talked about this transformation as "union with Christ." A variation of the expression "in Christ" occurs 216 times in Paul's writings and twenty-six times in the Johannine literature. It is an essential idea in the early church and is found (in different variations) in every major Christian theological tradition.

Yet rarely do we talk about "union with Jesus" as the purpose and goal of our spiritual lives. Rightfully, the idea of the Holy Spirit living inside us, and our lives being "hidden in Christ" (Colossians 3:3 NRSVue) might freak us out! But this is partly due to the Western emphasis on faith being more individualistic in nature, and more focused on *doing* than *being* categories. It also flows from the secular reduction of God from a living being we can be in relationship with, to an idea we can believe in.

Most descriptions of church refer to a place where Christians do our ritualistic stuff. But the Bible describes a community known for a quality of life together. The fruit of the Spirit for instance, "love, joy, peace, patience, kindness, generosity, faithfulness, gentleness, and self-control" (Galatians 5:22–23 NRSVue) flows from the communal nature of being "in Christ."

One way to understand this dynamic tension between place and community can be informed by a concept which first appeared with Aristotle (300s BCE) called *habitus*. Twentieth-century French sociologist Pierre Bourdieu greatly expanded the concept of habitus as a system of thought, perception, appreciation, and action.

We carry a system of dispositions, corporeal knowledge, beliefs, passions, and drives, in our bodies. This is a kind of second nature, or hardwiring, formed by story, parents, peers, and the repeated physicality of doing things which become habitual, reflexive, and embodied. Our body inhabits a social world, and that social world inhabits the body. This is our *habitus*.[3]

Historically, followers of Jesus have possessed a certain distinguishable habitus. In fact, Alan Kreider argues that through catechesis and worship, the primitive church was able to transform the habitus of those who were candidates for membership. This became a form of corporal nonconformity, an embodied way of life in community markedly different from the habitus of Roman society. This provides a window into the nature of the early church's communal life.

Consider how a small renegade movement, with no buildings or professional clergy, between the time of Jesus' death on the cross in the 30s and Constantine in the 300s, grew numerically across vast geographical distances. Kreider offers an extended analysis of what he terms "the improbable growth" of the early church in those days. He argues the most pronounced characteristics of that growth were the habitus of those early Christians, their embodied knowledge, and reflexive, bodily behavior, rooted in predispositions and expressed through practices. How they lived together—their habitus— this was their primary program of evangelism.[4]

More specifically, it was how Christians lived among outsiders. This was a key mark of early Christian habitus and the primary mode of their missional evangelism. Christians immersed themselves among the various social fields of Roman society. Early Christian worship was a mysterious closed gathering of the already catechized. Kreider writes, "It was not Christian worship that attracted outsiders; it was Christians who attracted them, and outsiders found the Christians attractive because of their Christian habitus, which catechesis and worship had formed."[5]

The early church formed people in the character of Christ. They experienced union with him and invited others into that union. It's hard not to notice that this approach is almost reversed in the US church. We emphasize attracting outsiders to a building where they can experience a worship service, rather than living out a distinct communal habitus in our daily lives. Most churches have no clear catechesis, and if they do, it's more about indoctrinating people in dogma than helping them experience and grow in union with Jesus.

How we go about growing in our relationship with the Risen Jesus, experiencing union with him, how we build community around him, all of this can be encapsulated by this one word . . . *together*.

A disciple of Jesus is someone who lives, loves, thinks, and acts like Jesus. This is the big idea of the word Christian, a "little Christ." That's a high bar, right? Perhaps we are never really truly a full-grown disciple, but we are in a lifelong journey of becoming one. This union with Jesus (being), is expressed in our habitus (daily living).

It seems that we have done well at making church members for our inherited denominational systems and networks, but have we formed people through communal life in Jesus? Do the metrics we employ measure union with Jesus and growth in his character? Or do they measure institutional affiliation? If the church was truly offering communal life in Jesus, would we be experiencing such a pronounced epidemic of loneliness and isolation?

We are living through a series of unfolding crises that are causing individual and collective harm on a massive scale. These overlapping crises include a global pandemic, systemic racism, climate change, political extremism, rising mental illness, an overdose epidemic, the proliferation of mass shootings, and the disintegration of genuine Christianity. I could add more to the list.

Any proposed framework for cultivating togetherness in the twenty-first century must be trauma-informed and centered in the compassion of Christ.

The consensus regarding the church among most so-called "nones and dones" (again these categories are built upon metrics that capture institutional affiliation, not a depth of communal life) is that amid these realities the church has been an instrument of further harm, not healing. The prevailing stereotype is that the church has added to the overall trauma of our age, through abuse, scandals, and moral failures. The church is known *not* to form people who live and love like Jesus.

Extended exposure to chronic mental and physical stress has evolved into collective trauma. Unresolved trauma is carried in our bodies, communities, and societal systems. If it goes unresolved it spills out in patterns of harm and is passed on intergenerationally. Again, as we say in the recovery fellowships, "Hurt people hurt people." In part II, we will explore a framework for how collective trauma can be resolved.

No one makes it through life unwounded. Every single one of us has been harmed, emotionally, physically, mentally, or spiritually. Some experience horrific levels of abuse that are completely debilitating. While there are varying degrees of trauma, every person has in some way been traumatized.

All wounds are not created equal, but all people are equally wounded.

A framework for cultivating healing communities of togetherness must embody the way, truth, and life of Jesus (John 14:6). It must be the embodiment of Christ's own compassion.

Together—Forever

The final act of salvation history is an ultimate portrait of togetherness. We could describe the center of this vision with two words . . . never alone.

We are never alone again. Revelation 21 and 22 transport us back to the future. Our future looks familiar. We are back in the garden. The tree of life is there. The river is there. We once again walk with God in "the cool of the day."

Godself wipes away every tear from our eyes. There is no more pain. There is no disease or suffering. There is no more war. There is no more gun violence. The leaves of the tree of life are "for the healing of the nations." We finally see that kingdom, where lambs and wolves lie down together, where lions eat straw like the ox, where the nations beat their swords into plowshares and their spears into pruning hooks.

Revelation 7 tells us that around the throne of the Lamb is a great multitude that no one can count, of every tribe and tongue, worshiping together in communion and love.

Let me tell you who else is there. My little brother, McKinley, sitting by the river of life, crystal clear, beneath the shade of the tree, beside our grandmother, beside all my friends who died in their addiction and their aching loneliness.

When my little brother was dying, and the medical team was easing me into the reality that he was essentially already gone, and I would need to pull the plug, a nurse asked Jill and me, "Are you his only family? This is going to be a big decision on your shoulders." Tears, like liquid prayers, streamed from my eyes as I nodded yes. "Well, he's lucky to have a person. Some people don't have one you know. You are his person."

I assume you are someone's person too. And I bet someone has been a person to you. It's likely if you've been around long enough, you have a person who is no longer here. The ultimate vision of the Christian faith is togetherness, with our persons, forever.

It is this weird, disturbing, almost inconceivable idea called the resurrection of the dead. That just as Jesus was raised from the dead in his flesh and blood body, the "first fruits" of the resurrection of the dead (1 Corinthians 15:20) so will each of us. So will every person who has ever died (Revelation 20:5–11).

However, this "good news for all people" doesn't only materialize in some post-mortem destiny. It begins right now. With the people right beside you. In the normal places where you do life together. Doing the normal things that you do. The promise is right there, you just have to seize the rope of hope God has thrown from the future, the anchor that is communal life in Jesus (Hebrews 6:19). It's a rope with a long reach, stretching back all the way to the beginning of our story. This is our *original unity*, the oneness we already are. The movement of communion with neighbor and all life.

In part II of the book, we will now turn to the practicality of cultivating healing communities of togetherness in a lonely world.

Part II

We are good by nature but corrupted by society.
—JEAN-JACQUES ROUSSEAU (1712–1778)

4

Compassionate Communities

How very good and pleasant it is
when kindred live together in unity!
—PSALM 133:1 (NRSVUE)

The automatic door chime goes off every couple minutes as new people trickle into Beauty in a Canvas tattoo parlor, on a Sunday afternoon. We start to circle up on the couches and floor space provided in the main waiting room. People are chatting, catching up since our last gathering, and introducing new friends that they brought along.

Some folks are up at the counter working with Ryan, our shop owner and main artist. They are sorting out what kind of ink they want, how big, and where on their bodies. Others are not getting tattoos today, and maybe never, but they like the vibe, the friendships, and the conversations. Here they have found *good* community, *compassionate* community.

After a while, things start to settle in and Angela, a relatively new believer, sleeved out with Christian iconography and Bible passages, asks a simple question, "So does anyone have a story behind one of your tattoos you want to share about today?" This initiates what we call "tattoo talks," a spiritual conversation around the memory and symbolism of our tattoos.

Gena shares about the African word *ubuntu* she got inked on her arm at Tattoo Parlor Church a couple years ago. "It reminds me that I am not alone, that I am a person through other persons, and this community is my safe place," Gena explains. Jason talks about the cover-up on his chest, a gang symbol he once received in prison, which is now the "shield of faith," from the whole armor of God passage in Ephesians 6.

Melanie shares about the handwriting on her forearm. It was the last note her deceased son Cody wrote to her before he overdosed on fentanyl. Kelly shares about the rainbow Jesus fish she had tattooed over the scars on her wrist. What once reminded her of an attempted suicide now reminds her that she is good and beloved.

Not all the stories are this profound. People laugh about the "tramp stamp" they got one night out clubbing on the boardwalk. There's the occasional poop emoji on the butt cheek, the result of a drunken spring break. An ex-spouse's name, or a college sports team that hasn't won in a while. Those stories are important too.

Some people share about the tattoo they are getting today. What it symbolizes. Why it is sacred to them. Why they want to inscribe it on their body for all eternity.

Yet as each person bravely tells their story, they are opening a window to their soul. They are being vulnerable in community with others. When they feel safe enough to share, they find mutuality and support.

The stories are innately spiritual in themselves. They are a spiritual autobiography of sorts, of where we have been, what we have been through, and where we are now. Some people in the circle would not identify as a Christian. Many label themselves as "spiritual but not religious." Some are interested in Eastern religions and others Native American spirituality. We sit together as a community of equals, sharing our truth.

Those who are Christians in the group bring their unique Jesus perspective on things to the circle. Why the teachings of Jesus have been meaningful to them. What spiritual practices help them flourish from day to day.

The conversation usually goes on for hours. When folks go back for their time in the artist chair, we cheer them on. Some regularly go back and snap pics of their friends getting inked, razzing them a bit about their pain threshold. When someone reemerges with a fresh tattoo, they show it to the group, we all clap and celebrate.

Some call getting ink, "tattoo therapy." This community sees tattoos as sacramental, an outward sign of an inward grace. We've been being church in a tattoo parlor for over a decade. Many find tattoos to be more than body art, but also a form of self-expression, healing, and self-acceptance. Ink therapy refers to victims of trauma and abandonment getting tattoos to heal their scars. It's intentionally submitting oneself to extensive pain for the sake of beauty.

This community sees their bodies as a "temple of the Holy Spirit" and their tattoos tell the story of Jesus and the church in stained glass.

Most of the people in Tattoo Parlor Church will never show up to our Sunday morning worship service, so we are being church with them where they do life. People like my little brother McKinley can find healing in this community. Indeed, part of our motivation for doing it these past ten years is so people like him don't have to die alone of a broken heart.

Perhaps this idea is pretty radical for you, and you're thinking "Yeah tattoo church would never be *my* thing." I absolutely understand that.

So let's return to my friend Olive from the introduction, the one who died alone in a nursing home, primarily abandoned by her family, and the church she gave her life to. Join me in the Brookdale Senior Living Center for another kind of church. This one gathers every Monday afternoon. A group of senior saints who have transitioned into this assisted living facility circle up for a time of prayer, check in, and sermonic conversation. They call the group Shenanigans, because they are intent on stirring up holy mischief together.

Some of the chief mischief makers are our church members at St. Marks UMC in Ocala, who became residents. They have faithfully given their prayers, presence, gifts, service, and witness to the church, some for many decades. They can't get to the sanctuary on Sunday mornings anymore, so our team goes to be church with them where they live.

There's no official sermon during this time, but like Tattoo Parlor Church there is a spiritual dialogue. Group members share honestly about the joys and struggles in their lives. They report highlights like visits from grandkids, and they mourn loved ones they haven't seen in a while. They process together when someone in the community dies. They clasp hands and pray together.

Unfortunately, bad theology really does kill. Let me explain what I mean.

Sociologists have long distinguished between extrinsic religiosity and intrinsic religiosity.[1] Extrinsic religiosity is motivated by how religion can be used to satisfy one's own needs. People in this space see religious participation as a means to achieve security, social status, social connectedness, and so on.

These extrinsic types turn to God without turning away from the self and use religion toward their own ends. Intrinsic religiosity, in contrast, is motivated by guiding principles for how to live with integrity and a meaning-endowed framework.

Gordon Allport and J Michael Ross punctuate the distinction as follows, "The extrinsically motivated person *uses* their religion, whereas the intrinsically motivated *lives* their religion."[2] Dr. Monika Ardelt has done significant research on wisdom, spirituality, ageing well, dying well, and the effects of spiritual community. Dr. Ardelt has developed a culturally inclusive Three-Dimensional Wisdom Model that contains cognitive, reflective, and compassionate (affective) dimensions. She is the creator of the widely used Three-Dimensional Wisdom Scale (3D-WS), synthesizing both Western and Eastern approaches to offer a definition and conceptualization of wisdom as an integration of these three dimensions.[3]

Her work gives us a valid instrument to measure wisdom, compassion, and the power of spiritual community. While spirituality is not a science, in some sense we can assess spirituality in a scientific way. For example, some of her research has been specifically with seniors in assisted living facilities and hospice. In one such study, Ardelt and Koenig utilize the concepts of extrinsic and intrinsic religiosity to assess participants' sense of purpose in life, well-being, and death attitudes. They found extrinsic religiosity had a negative indirect effect on a sense of purpose in life and was directly related to greater death anxiety.[4]

They also discovered that people high on intrinsic religiosity, who lean into spiritual activities, have a higher sense of purpose in life, subjective well-being, and less death anxiety. In this study, an individual's religious orientation did indeed have positive and negative effects on their overall well-being.

Participation in spiritual activities was measured with "participation with at least one other person and frequency of prayer."[5] Further studies with the ageing demonstrate that intrinsic religiosity leads to better health outcomes, deeper meaning and purpose, and peaceful death acceptance in older adults. Whereas extrinsic religiosity leads to decline in health outcomes and greater death anxiety.[6]

Not surprisingly, individuals who reported inconsistency between religious beliefs and religious behaviors also reported the highest levels of death anxiety. Ardelt and Koenig discovered that intrinsic religious orientation was positively related to shared spiritual activities with at least one person, such as Bible study, church attendance, and frequency of prayer. The individuals who participated in shared spiritual activities were also more likely to spend time in prayer. By contrast, those of the extrinsic religious orientation were less likely to participate in shared spiritual activities. Increased time in prayer also reduced death anxiety.[7]

These findings indicate that spiritual activities with at least one other person and an active prayer life are particularly important for nursing home residents in promoting subjective well-being and reducing fear of death. However, the challenge is that intrinsically religious nursing home residents encounter more obstacles to engaging in spiritual activities than those not in an assisted living facility. Furthermore, residents who were in shared room arrangements had the additional challenge of lack of privacy and space for a contemplative prayer life.[8] In other words, plenty of isolation, but no space for solitude.

Collectively these studies suggest that nursing home staff should offer religious and spiritual activities to promote subjective well-being and decrease death anxiety among their residents, but the spiritual care must be contextualized for each person. Providing a "sacred space" for intrinsically religious nursing home residents is essential to their spiritual well-being. Even a small spiritual community of two people can significantly increase overall wellness and peace at the end of life.[9] Collectively, this research validates scientifically the power of spiritual community.

"It is not good for the man to be alone" (Genesis 2:18). And it is not good for people to die alone. A small community like Shenanigans can have profound positive impacts on overall well-being for people in the later stages of life.

Bad theology kills because it leads to negative religious coping which flows from distorted beliefs. People's perceptions of God—punishing, judgmental, absent, or dishing out suffering for some greater purpose—led to poorer health outcomes and self-defeating behaviors. Our theology, how we think about God, suffering, and death, affects every dimension of our humanity and greater well-being. It also impacts our compassion response, our ability to empathize and care for others. It even enhances or diminishes our desire for community itself.

What kind of religiosity do you think dominates in the American context? Studies indicate that we have largely formed people for extrinsic religiosity that does not lead to increased compassion response and prosocial behaviors.[10] A personal and individualistic faith, which de-emphasizes the power of communal life. This is an extrinsic orientation that forces us to live in a state of dualistic thinking and hypocrisy. Turning to God without turning away from the false self, or toward our neighbor. Professing belief in a spirituality of compassion, while not living it.

When one in three Americans have experienced religious trauma, and the leading cause of people distancing themselves from the church is the harmful behavior of Christians, it's increasingly unlikely people will show up on Sunday mornings to attend our inherited services.

This is why compassionate communities must form in the everyday spaces and rhythms of life. They must discard the harmful aspects of toxic theology, meet people where they are, and start where the good news starts, by affirming the goodness and sacred worth of every person. Communities where we nurture people in "self-compassion," which sociologist Kristin Neff, developer of the Self-Compassion Scale (SCS), describes as having three core components:

1. Self-kindness: that we be gentle and understanding with ourselves rather than harshly critical and judgmental.
2. Recognition of common humanity: that we feel connected with others in the experience of life rather than feeling isolated and alienated by our suffering.
3. Mindfulness: that we hold our experience in balanced awareness, rather than ignoring our pain or exaggerating it.[11]

Consider the extraordinarily high rates of burnout and compassion fatigue among people in helping professions. The rate of pastors quitting the ministry profession is alarming. Some of the healthiest clergy leaders I work with who stay in ministry for the long haul have learned to practice self-compassion. They integrate it into their prayer practice. They begin by letting Jesus speak words of affirmation over them, they recognize the pitfalls of ministry are beyond their control, and from this awareness, they "let go and let God."

In the recovery fellowships we have "Rule 62," which is "don't take yourself too damn seriously." This ability to stay "right-sized" is essential to the practice of self-compassion.

The missing "good" in the good news

My friend Tracy openly shares about the harm she experienced at the hands of Christians as an LGBTQ person. She was restricted from working with children, and ultimately cast out of the church because of her sexual orientation. For her, the church only had bad news to share. You are bad, your behvaior is bad, your personhood is bad. Fortunately, Tracy was able to not give up on a church that gave up on her. Today she is actively cultivating a fresh expression called Midweek Grind, a safe space for LGBTQ persons to explore spirituality in a local coffee shop.[12] Remember, Fresh Expressions of Church are forms of church for people not connected to the more traditional modes. They gather in the normal spaces and rythmns of daily life.

Whether we are young, old, or somewhere in between, the gospel of Jesus Christ affirms over us the same core conviction . . . we are very good. This is God's first word to us, and it is the starting point of our theology. The goodness that we already are.

Thomas Merton describes the struggle of the soul with self-hatred and unworthiness, and how when we live in that state, we will view others through the same distorted lens. This is why the commandment to believe is prior to the commandment to love. Merton writes, "The root of Christian love is not the will to love, but *the faith that one is loved*. The faith that one is loved *by God*. That faith that one is loved by God although unworthy—or, rather, irrespective of one's worth!"[13]

The creation story does not begin with how terrible humanity is, how utterly helpless we are to do anything about it. It begins with human beings made in the image of a good God, created for relationship with God and one another. A people who are loved by God.

Yes, that's not the whole picture, as we have explored in the second movement . . . *Alone*. However, let's recall God's conversation with Cain, "Sin is lurking at the door; its desire is for you, *but you must master it*" (Genesis 4:7 NRSVue, italics mine). This communicates at least a hope in the heart of God, that we will choose the good. That empowered by the Spirit, we can master the sin impulses that lead to the harm of ourselves and others. That we really can answer Cain's question, "Am I my brother's keeper?" in the affirmative. Yes, we are to love our siblings, to tend the life-giving relationships that make us whole.

In *The Compassionate Instinct: The Science of Human Goodness*, Dacher Keltner writes, "So we might think about compassion as a biologically based skill or virtue, but not one we either have or don't have. Instead, it's a trait that we can develop in an appropriate context."[14] Keltner presents research that suggests compassion is an evolved part of our human nature, rooted in our brain and biology, and ready to be cultivated for the common good.

There is a growing scientific and clinical interest in understanding how compassion can be cultivated. This has led to compassion training programs like the Compassion Cultivation Training (CCT) designed at Stanford University. Researchers suggest compassion is a key component of individual, interpersonal, organizational, and societal well-being. They suggest compassion is a fundamental skill that can be trained. "Cultivating compassion may contribute to sustained well-being in individuals, groups, and organizations."[15]

Every person has the capacity for compassion and Fresh Expressions can provide the "appropriate context" for its formation and flourishing. Spiritual leaders are utilizing these scientific breakthroughs in the cultivation of these communities.

You're utterly bad, you're helplessly evil, and there's nothing you can do about it. That sounds like bad news to me, and it sounds bad to at least the last four generations of human beings, the "nones and dones" who have left the church *en masse*. In fact, it's as if we have omitted an entire movement in the three-part act of salvation. Good. Alone. Together. But we leave off the *good* part.

I suspect most people see in themselves some vestige of goodness, some tendency to choose love. We are literally wired for that. Doing evil, doing harm, takes intentional effort. We must fight the goodness baked into our molecules to do wrong. Of course, I suspect most people also know we have a significant track record of exactly, willfully, doing the wrong thing. Unless some kind of mental illness is blocking our capacity to feel guilt, to care about others, to desire to see them flourish. We are mostly good, although significantly wounded and in need of healing grace.

I want to suggest that compassionate communities are inclusive, and they start where God starts, with the goodness that every person already is. After all, as Paul reminds us, it's the kindness of God that leads you to repentance (Romans 2:4). Affirming the sacred worth of every person is the starting place of a trauma-informed, compassion-centered community. What we are doing sitting around in that circle on the floor of a tattoo parlor, or in the day room of the assisted care facility, is helping ground ourselves in our core identity as God's beloved, healing false self-images and harmful God-images.

The starting point of our journey as Christians is to open ourselves to God's unconditional love. Before we were flesh and blood, we were a vision in the imagination of a good God. The psalmist realizes this condition, writing, "I praise you because I am fearfully and wonderfully made; your works are wonderful, I know that full well" (Psalm 139:14).

God knitted every person together in love. God formed each of us as a one-of-a-kind masterpiece. All our lives, God has been pursuing us. Even when we were unaware, God was wooing, calling, and desiring a relationship with us.

I remember when Kayleigh, a twenty-four year old single mother with two little ones, made this realization at Burritos and Bibles (B&B). She had previously had a harmful experience of church as a child, but showed up to Moe's Southwest Grill at the invitation of a friend. At B&B, we eat great burritos and have spiritual conversations. We conclude the gathering with the Lord's Supper, taking, blessing, breaking and sharing the tortilla, and passing around a chalice filled with Hi C from the Coke machine. After months of attending, Kayleigh experienced the grace of God in a sustained and profound way. She responded with a desire to be baptized.

This is why the starting point of our entrance into a compassionate community is typically baptism. Our baptism is a way to respond to God's loving act of creation and reconciliation. In our baptism, we experience a mini-death of the false self as we are submerged, trickled, or splashed with water. In the waters, we die with Christ. Jesus teaches us in the Sermon on the Mount that to be "poor in spirit" is to be blessed. It's not those who are perfect or powerful who are blessed. Jesus says, "Blessed are the meek," for they will "inherit the earth" (Matthew 5:1–3, 5).

Meekness is not weakness. It is "strength under control." Jesus, for example, is meekness embodied. The one in whom the fullness of God was pleased to dwell emptied himself by taking the form of a servant (Colossians 1:19; Philippians 2:6–7).

Baptism is an acknowledgment of the universal human condition of "poverty of spirit." We acknowledge that we are wounded and infected with the virus of in-being sin, and we need God to heal us and take over the management of our lives (Romans 7:18). Only from that confession of need, through repentance, can we enter rightly into a relationship with God. We like the prodigal child have run away, come to the end of ourselves, and turn to find ourselves wrapped in unconditional love (see Luke 15:17).

Those grace-filled waters are also a sign of our resurrection. We emerge as a new creation. One aspect of this new creation is our union with Christ. We are now "in Christ" and Christ is in us.

Our baptism is a way to recognize and affirm what God is doing in us. Through it we claim our birthright, our identity as God's beloved. The innate goodness that was already there is being renewed. The wound of original trauma is being healed.

Before we did anything, right or wrong, great or terrible, God spoke over us . . . *beloved*! God's first word to us is "You are my beloved, with whom I am well pleased."

For those of us who grew up without one or both parents, something deep inside of us longs to hear these words. The wound of a compassionless childhood is deforming to the soul. We will sometimes go to great lengths to try to earn our worthiness, to prove we too are beloved. It's the burning obsession of my life to help others believe that for themselves, but if I'm honest, it remains much harder to embrace for myself. In fact, I tattooed "beloved" over the scars on my arm. It reminds me who I am on the days I don't believe it. It is a tool to help me move towards self-compassion.

When we live from the place of God's belovedness, we can truly love others.

Belovedness, "very goodness," is at the core of our identity. God loves you just as you are, not as you should be. Only in a community where we can truly be human can real discipleship take place.

When we weave some version of this message into the dialogue in our fresh expressions of church, many people who hear it for the first time get emotional. Your soul can feel that it is good and right. It's a truth that resonates in our bones. Sadly, it's not a message the church has been known for.

Our Christian attempts at evangelization have come off as one-dimensional and out of touch. What many people hear in the message of the church is that there's a really good God who created really bad people, but Jesus came to save us in spite of how jacked up we are. God the Father punishes the hell out of God the Son on the cross, so we don't have to go to hell when we die. Rather, we will go to a beautiful cloud city called heaven, or at least our soul will (maybe Greek Gnosticism did win the day after all). All we have to do is have a Christian pray us through the "Romans Road," leading us through the sinner's prayer, as we accept Jesus Christ as our personal Lord and Savior.

Don't forget the political and financial benefits if you accept this intellectual proposition. Jesus is fully sided with whatever political party you affiliate with. He actually hates the other side, who are all liars and thieves and will likely burn in the lake of fire for all eternity.

I mean that sounds like a hell of a deal, right? Nice and easy. Especially because most of the people who represent this message don't live much differently than anybody else. Jesus is a fascinating, compassion-filled person, who seemed to love and heal everyone he encountered, except those couple run-ins with the religious leaders. From an outsider perspective

Christians don't live anything like him. What do you have to lose?

I'm being facetious here, but this is a recurring theme in our fresh expressions conversations with people who don't go to church. In fact, outsiders are skeptical of this whole scheme. First, why would we ever want to worship a God who creates some people destined for eternal hell, while others use their Get Out of Jail Free card by saying a magic prayer? What kind of Father would punish the hell out of their innocent Son?

One challenge here is that evangelistic tactics many Christians have used for the last fifty years are fear-based and shallow. We also assume a worldview that has been widely rejected. We are simply answering questions that emerging generations are not asking. Think about it. When is the last time a young person approached you with a concerned look, and said, "Can you help me not go to hell when I die?" Not sure about you, but no one at any point in my life has ever asked me that question.

"I feel lonely sometimes." "I'm struggling with a behavior that I know I shouldn't be doing, how do I stop?" "It seems no one really cares about me, am I unlovable?" "Is there more to life than making money and having a big following on social media?" "I think I've been queer since my earliest childhood memories, is there a place for me?" "Are there a people I can be myself with, to be known and loved?" These are some questions I hear a lot. And the good news is, Jesus has an actual answer for each one of these questions.

Jesus' message had little to do with not going to hell when we die. There are a few teachings where he leans heavily into the apocalyptic stuff, but his message was much more this-worldly than going around selling an escape hatch from a bummer of a post-mortem destiny.

Consider some of the following questions Jesus asked . . .

- "Do you want to be made well?" "Do you have faith I can heal you?"
- "You have all the law stuff down, now can you be like the good Samaritan, and be filled with compassion for your neighbor?"
- "And if you greet your brethren only, what is unusual about that? Do not the unbelievers do the same?"
- "Can any of you by worrying add a single moment to your lifespan?" "Why are you anxious about clothes?"
- "Why do you notice the splinter in your brother's eye yet fail to perceive the wooden beam in your own?"
- "Do people pick grapes from thorn bushes or figs from thistles?"
- "Why are you terrified?" "Why do you harbor evil thoughts? Clear that junk out."
- "Which of you who has a sheep that falls into a pit on the Sabbath will not take hold of it and lift it out?"
- "Who is my mother? Who are my brothers? This community of disciples is my family."
- "Why did you doubt?"
- "And why do you break the commandments of God for the sake of your tradition?"
- "Who do people say the Son of Man is? But who do you say that I am?"
- "What profit would there be for one to gain the whole world and forfeit their life and what can one give in exchange for their life?"

I could keep going, as there are like three hundred more of those! They all sound very this-worldly to me. Jesus has a word of healing for our anxiety, our fears, our shame, our loneliness. "Believe in me and you'll not go to hell when you die," was simply *not* Jesus' message. "If anyone wants to follow after me, they must deny themselves, take up their cross, and follow me"—that was the actual heart of Jesus' message. "If you choose to yoke with me, I'll walk beside you, I'll even carry you at times. You'll need to leave the false self behind. But if you mess up, we will start over—yes, Peter, even if it's three times! I'll restore you back three times."

You will know shalom . . . peace. In your world and in yourself. I will make you whole. You belong to me, and I belong to you. Abide in me, and I'll abide in you. I'll grow fruit on your tree, fruit that will last. Yes, there are lots of regulations, but just do this . . . love God, love neighbor, the rest will come out in the wash. Forgive each other, like I've forgiven you.

"I will never leave you nor forsake you." Come whatever may. You will never be *alone* again.

That was the heart of the good news according to Jesus.

Perhaps, if we want to help people find healing from isolation and the pain of loneliness, we should, like Jesus, ask more questions than we give answers. Perhaps we should discover what are the actual questions people are asking, and how Jesus is the answer. This requires a massive act of repentance, *metanoia*, a turning in a new direction, theologically and ecclesiologically.

Becoming good guests

Let's walk through the blueprint for cultivating compassionate communities by exploring Luke 9 and 10. Then we will zoom in on Luke 10:1–9. In both chapters Jesus sends the disciples out two by two. He orients them to the situation, instructing them to prayerfully attend the context. "The harvest is plentiful, the laborers are few; therefore ask the Lord of the harvest" (Luke 10:2 NRSVue).

In Luke 9, Jesus deploys the twelve "sent ones" to become an extension of himself. They are to do the very things Jesus is doing in the power of the Holy Spirit: to heal, liberate, and proclaim the kingdom. They are like rays of traveling light . . . divine energy, healing presence, embodied compassion.

This is on-the-job training. It's as if Jesus is saying, *All right, you've watched me long enough, now go do what I'm doing, then let's process how that goes.* No ten years of preparatory education, ordination process, and seminary here. Notice that Jesus doesn't tell them to build buildings and stick up signs announcing service times. In going out in teams, they are being the church, announcing the reign of God breaking into the normal spaces and rhythms of life.

There is not just one Jesus now but twelve, and the often-unmentioned women, laboring in the background behind the curtain of patriarchy (Luke 8:1–3). They are his body, multiplied. They are the embodiment of his own divine life in miniature. Notice that he also tells them to travel light, in that they must leave all the clutter of extra possessions behind. This requires trust; it is a journey of faith. *Just go out there, I'll meet your needs* (Luke 9:1–6).

This is an important word for the church today. We usually show up on the scene with our head and hands full, thinking we have the answers and solutions for those we are sent to. The Jesus posture requires humility, mutuality, and listening. We need the people we are sent to more than they need us. Mission across history has done harm when carried out in a narrative of ennoblement, power, and domination. Missionaries went in the spirit of expansion, supported by empire to claim new peoples and territories for God. That is mission in *the name of Jesus* but not in *the way of Jesus*.

This posture also requires us to leave behind our emotional and theological baggage. How can we be healers when we ourselves aren't healthy? How can we provide answers when we don't know what questions our neighbors are asking? What harmful self and God images do we carry into conversations that might cause harm?

Contextual theology is co-created in the process of relationship and mutual listening. It is not about going in and making people believe the way we do. It starts with understanding what people believe and creating a dialogue of equal exchange.

In fresh expressions, we call this a *belonging before believing* way of being church. Historically, the church has followed the pattern of *believe, behave, belong*. First, if you believe, publicly recite the creed, renounce the spiritual forces of wickedness, do the membership class, then you can join us. Congratulations, you are a member now, with all rights and privileges stipulated therein. However, you must now behave . . . acting, thinking, and voting like the rest of us. If not, we will pull the 1 Corinthians "expel the immoral person" card on you (1 Corinthians 5:11–13). If you behave well enough, long enough, then you can belong. Then you can be one of us.

In fresh expressions we reverse that process. You could think of it as a modified version of this sequence: *belong, believe, behave*. We create communities of belonging first. Believing comes along at the pace of grace, or maybe never at all.

For example, we have a self-professed atheist in one of our communities. Wayne shows up faithfully, makes coffee, sets up, cleans up. He is endearingly called the "coffee warden" by some, as he does have a tendency to count how many cups people drink. I often say, "Wayne, the coffee is free, let it flow! Jesus can turn water into wine after all!" Recently, Wayne had a brief hospitalization. In our recovery church, I told him, "Wayne, listen to your damn doctor, we love and need you around here!" Then we asked him if the community could circle up and pray. He broke down weeping hysterically as we laid hands on him.

Whether Wayne ever believes like I do or not, my role is to foster a compassionate community where Wayne can belong. The final piece, *behave*, is not a primary concern. It's the Holy Spirit's job to do behavior modification, not mine, and not yours. The only exception is when there is harmful behavior that threatens to wound people in the community. Then as group leaders we must have hard conversations and confront that behavior.

In essence, we create communities where we can experience true belonging, and we live out our beliefs in relationship together. This is a way to embody Jesus' instructions to travel light in the twenty-first century.

Back to Luke. The "sent ones" return to process their work. Jesus takes them away for a time of rest and reflection. However, the crowds discover their location and disrupt the time of solitude. We see a pattern here. Periods of highly impactful social activity, intentional time of solitude. Even when the world breaks into the wilderness, Jesus always responds with compassion (Luke 9:10–17).

"Send these hungry people away, Lord!" the disciples demand. "You feed them," Jesus responds. Rather than simply solving the problem for them, he invites them to be a part of the solution. Some have called this *adaptive leadership*. Giving the work back to the people. Helping them discover their own inner resources to meet the challenge. Distributing power equally among the community.

Then Jesus drops the bombshell: "I'm going to suffer and die." Biblical scholars believe this is the hinge point in Luke's gospel. It's all uphill—heading towards Jerusalem—from here. The cross looms on the horizon (Luke 9:18–27).

But, wait, there's more: ". . . and you also must carry your cross to follow me." This is Jesus' invitation to a cruciform life. A self-emptying (kenotic) life of downward mobility. A life of service to others. A life of compassion.

We don't have to look far to see just how countercultural this cruciform way of life is. In a consumeristic society we are programmed to reduce life to a series of commodities and transactions. We suck the world dry of its resources to feed our every desire. We even commoditize human lives. We prioritize individual rights over relationships and sacrifice our children on the altar of the "right to bear arms." And we legitimize all of this through a false and corrupt form of Christianity. Armed Christian nationalists show up to support criminal politicians whose legislative power is funded by firearm manufacturers and pharmaceutical companies.

Perhaps the church in the United States has, in the words of Jesus, "lost our soul to gain the whole world." We have become known as an exclusive and even harmful group, rather than an inclusive and compassion-centered one.

As we follow the triumphant processional of a nonviolent, peasant, donkey-riding Messiah with no army to his death-conquering confrontation with the principalities and powers, may it be an opportunity to reevaluate our lives and communities.

Next, Jesus takes a handful of disciples up on the mountain. He is transfigured before them. They catch a glimpse of the fullness of who Jesus is. There stand Moses and Elijah, signifying that Jesus himself is the fulfillment of the law and the prophets. This is a key emphasis of Luke's gospel.

Peter's first instinct is to commemorate and institutionalize this moment. "Let's build structures and stay here forever!" A voice from heaven hushes Peter's impulse and says, "This is my beloved, listen up!" Then Jesus leads them down from the mountaintop into the valley where great crowds are waiting with their seemingly unending needs. An afflicted child, hungry people, disciples competing for greatness and getting territorial about outsiders casting out demons in Jesus' name (Luke 9:28–48).

In the Christendom form of the church, we have largely sought to be a church on the mountaintop. We build grand structures. We gather people in those spaces to experience a moment of transfiguration. We confess again together that Jesus is Lord. We announce what's happening and invite people to join us. We are always playing host. Come to us, we will host you here, at a time we have chosen, in ritual ways we have predetermined.

As much as we love the mountaintop moments of transfiguration, our solitude is lived out in the pain and struggle of the valley. We can't set up shop and live in the seclusion of spiritual ecstasy. I'm grateful for the clarity of the transfiguration event. As Merton reminds us, solitude is not separation. We go into the desert not to escape other people, but to find them in God. "There is no solitude except interior solitude. And interior solitude is not possible for anyone who does not accept his right place in relation to others."[16]

And yet, we already start to see fragmenting among these first Christians, "Lord, we saw outsiders healing in your name; we tried to stop them, because they're not with us!" Here we see perhaps the first case of *odium theologicum*—hatred for those nearby who are religiously similar to oneself but none-theless different.

Can Jesus' words slice through history and cut us to the heart today? "Do not stop them; for whoever is not against you is for you." Such is life in the valley. While we are in a state of transfiguration, society in general goes on in a narrative of conquest, exceptionalism, violence, and dualistic us-against-them thinking. This is why we must spend a significant block of time every day to sit in silence and adore the transfigured face of Jesus. To see Jesus in the face of every neighbor. It gives us the self-compassion to live on in the valley.

By Luke 10, Jesus is sending out seventy disciples (or seventy-two depending on our translation). The community has multiplied from twelve to seventy—enough disciples to cover the seventy nations named in Genesis 10—that is, the world. There is not just one Jesus, but many, each a microcosm of his own human/divine life. The birth of an indestructible community called the body of Christ.

Jesus sees the multitudes, harassed and helpless, because the shepherds of the day were asleep on the job. "First, pray, ask the Lord of the harvest." Where some would see insurmountable challenge, Jesus sees endless possibility. *Now, put sneakers on your prayers, go!* The disciples are sent out in teams of three, two by two, led by the Spirit. They must travel light, trust God, and risk life and limb like lambs among wolves (Luke 10:1–3).

Most importantly they must locate *persons of peace*, those welcomers who open the community and invite them to their tables. There they must "eat whatever is set before you"—theological validation for the potluck! Do life with those people. Love and serve. Build relationships. Then and only then . . . heal, bless, proclaim the kingdom (Luke 10:5–9).

Here we have Jesus' missional blueprint for a pre-Christian world. But might it also be a blueprint for a post-Christian world? Is it not obvious that the harvest is plentiful, but the laborers are few in the twenty-first century? Luke 10 shows us an anciently fresh way to follow Jesus in the twenty-first century.

One of the most glaring questions Luke forces us to ask is how did we get from this to what the church is today? There are no buildings, no safety, no sticking up a sign and saying, "All are welcome." The community of disciples is sent out into a plentiful harvest field to be the church. We are not the hosts but rather the guests.

The church in the West has been able to play host for centuries. You come to us. Into our space at a time we have determined. To worship in a way we have already decided before you get here. We have hospitality programs, hospitality training, and a hospitality team. But Jesus didn't instruct us to be good *hosts*, he instructed us to be good *guests*.

Notice the posture of vulnerability and mutuality. We are completely dependent on the ones we are sent to. No narrative of colonial expansion and dispossession of natives here. Rather, it's a command to rediscover the "oneness we already are" and to "have the same love" (Philippians 2:2)—embrace the customs, food, and rhythms of the people we are sent to, in the spaces where we do life together.

Perhaps as we see the decline and irrelevancy of the church in the West, we could reframe it as a moment of massive opportunity—an opportunity to truly be the church Jesus designed, equipped, and empowered us to be. Truly, the harvest is plentiful, and the laborers are few.

Keltner insightfully states, "Human communities are only as healthy as our conceptions of human nature."[17] We are bearers of good news, sent to good people, to cultivate compassionate communities, where people experience healing. The work of communal formation requires transparency, safety, and sensitivity to self and others. And *compassionate* communities must be *real* communities.

Real Communities

*Therefore confess your sins to each other and
pray for each other so that you may be healed.*
—JAMES 5:16

Why are you alone? I want to know why you're alone?"
questions Danny frantically, standing up on the stage
of an old theater which is scheduled to soon be demolished.

Danny, a filmmaker, has assembled a group of his single
friends for a Valentine's Day "party." Suddenly, a film crew
appears from behind the curtain and Danny begins to question each person live on camera. Each participant begins to
get real about their lives, failed relationships, intimacy issues,
and loneliness.

Why are *you* alone? How would you answer that question?

The strange plotline of the Henry Jaglom film *Someone
to Love* (1987) takes another odd turn when Orson Welles
appears in the back row of the theater and begins pontificating. Once the credits begin to roll, Welles comes on screen and
says, "We're born alone, we live alone, we die alone. Only
through our love and friendship can we create the illusion for

the moment that we're not alone."[1] Welles was communicating a core assumption that the film was grappling with, and his words have become immortalized in popular culture.

Orson Welles was an American director, actor, writer, and producer, widely considered to be among the greatest and most influential filmmakers of all time. His radio broadcasts, theater plays, and films helped shape a generation who turned to movie screens for their legitimating narratives. Welles was less offering an original idea than he was naming a prevailing sociocultural assumption of Western individualism. Is Welles articulating something true? Are momentary glimpses of community and connection not real, merely an illusion? Are we ultimately and truly alone?

"Love is our true destiny. We do not find the meaning of life by ourselves alone—we find it with another," writes Thomas Merton, born just a few months before Welles in 1915. We have been drawing on the work of Merton throughout this book. His reflections on the contemplative life have been massively impactful in the twentieth century. While inhabiting the same century, and both influential in their own way, these two men seem to have very different perspectives.

Merton reflects, in *Conjectures of a Guilty Bystander*, an experience he had standing on a crowded street corner:

In Louisville, at the corner of 4th [now Muhammad Ali Blvd.] and Walnut, in the center of the shopping district, I was suddenly overwhelmed with the realization that I loved all those people, that they were mine and I theirs, that we could not be alien to one another even though we were total strangers. . . . This changes nothing in the sense and value of my solitude, for it is, in fact, the function of solitude to make one realize such things with a clarity that would be impossible to one completely immersed in other cares. . . . My solitude, however, is not my own. It is because I am one with them that I owe it to them to be alone, and when I am alone, they are not "they" but my own self. There are no strangers. . . . If only we could see each other that way all the time. . . . But this cannot be seen, only believed and 'understood' by a peculiar gift."[2]

One essential aspect of Merton's thinking is a vision of "the oneness we already are." In October 1968, only weeks before his tragic and mysterious death by electrocution through a faulty fan wire in his room, Merton shared at a Calcutta conference before a large audience of Asian monks: "My dear brothers, we are already one. But we imagine that we are not. What we have to recover is our original unity. What we have to be is what we are."[3]

In *New Seeds of Contemplation*, now considered a classic in spiritual literature, Merton lays out various aspects of contemplative life. As we have seen, Merton emphasizes that true contemplation is not about striving to achieve union with God but recognizing the union that already exists within us. How he describes the self in union with God counters the privatized and individualized spirituality that dominates today. For Merton, Christian spirituality is not a private "me-and-God" relationship. It is ultimately a communal vision that restores us to *original unity*.

The Christian life is a journey of living out the reality of our truest self, made in the image of God. A self that is created to live in loving union with God and others. The spiritual journey of knowing God is inextricably bound with the discovery of our true self. . . our authentic identity in God. Merton describes three stages of the journey of spiritual transformation as awakening from the false self, searching for the true self, and union with God's self.[4]

1. *Awakening from false self.* The first movement is the turn from superficiality to authenticity. The path to true self begins with the awareness that we are "shadowed by an illusory person: a false self."[5] The distorted and false self results from the fragmentation and fallout of sin—a perceived state of isolation. The movement from the false to the true self is more an ongoing journey than a destination.

2. *Search for the true self.* This describes the path of finding our reality in God. It is an intentional response to the calling of God which usually requires some form of spiritual discipline that is lived out in an ongoing way. Merton sees contemplation as a way of life, not merely a form of prayer. Through it we co-create the truth of our identity in God, discovering ultimately that "Love is my true identity. Selflessness is my true self. Love is my true character. Love is my name."[6]

3. *Union with God's self.* This describes the process of differentiation between our true identity and the false self. "I must learn to 'leave myself' in order to find myself by yielding to the love of God." In this movement we recognize the harm caused by living in the false self, to ourselves, to others, and to creation itself. Union is a healing identification process, "infused contemplation" of sheer grace. Describing union with God, Merton says, "God alone is left. He is the 'I' who acts there. He is the one Who loves and knows and rejoices."[7] It is also here that "in my soul

and in your soul I find the same Christ Who is our
Life, and He finds Himself in our love, and together
we all find Paradise, which is the sharing of His Love
for His Father in the Person of Their Spirit."[8]

Walter Edwards is a man who made this journey. I
approached him at a clergy gathering about twenty years ago
and asked him if he would be my mentor. There was something unique about his presence. He was quiet, reserved, but
when he spoke you could tell it was coming from a deep well.
I could see in him something lacking in myself, although I
couldn't articulate it then.

Walter took me under his wing when I was a new pastor
trying to figure out ministry. We met weekly until his death
three years ago. Slowly, prayerfully, he asked questions that
made me reflect deeply about my own motivations and spiritual development. Walter had left behind the false self long
ago, he was fully who he was, and his personhood was completely interdependent with God. His aura was love. There
were times when Walter was speaking, that God was literally
speaking through him. What was his secret? Walter introduced
me to solitude, the practice of contemplative prayer. Even in
death he guides me now in my ongoing search for true self.

The false and superficial self is like a parody of our true self.
Its unrealness seeks to prove itself real through constant validation and visibility. Social media is an ideal breeding ground
for the false self to thrive, one in which "likes," "loves," and
"shares" fuel the momentary illusion of realness. The false self
has its origin in that first deceptive serpent question where
we started our journey, "Did God really say?" The question
belies a lack of proximity with God. God is other and sepa-
rate, withholding something good from us. Once we accept

the illusion, we move into gradual degrees of isolation, fleeing, hiding, concealing, and blaming (Genesis 3).

Merton's idea of the union with God's self in the solitude of contemplation is not about withdrawal from the world. "Go into the desert not to escape other men but in order to find them in God."[9] This union is embodied in the context of relationships and in everyday life. Discovering our true self leads us into deeper levels of union with one another and the world. Becoming real to ourselves and to God enables the possibility to be real to others. It reconnects us to the original unity.

Thus, the need to further distinguish isolation and solitude. Isolation is a sin instinct. Solitude is a holiness instinct. "True solitude is the home of the person, false solitude the refuge of the individualist."[10] We need the space of solitude in the stillness of retreat, so we can live more fully from the true self with our family, friends, coworkers, and neighbors. "Contemplation is out of the question for anyone who does not try to cultivate compassion for other men. For Christianity is not merely a doctrine or system of beliefs, it is Christ living in us and uniting us to one another in His own Life and unity."[11] The discovery of true self leads us in loving service to the people who are also all part of the "oneness we already are."

So then a spirituality of compassion is the way of true self. It is a sensitivity to the suffering in ourselves and others. It does not draw back from the suffering. It does not merely wish the suffering away or ignore it. We stay with it, feel it, as God stays with it, feels it. We move into the pain of fragmentation and loneliness in real ways, so we can create real healing. Real community. Original unity.

The prevailing individualistic narrative that Welles was naming is quite wrong. His perception of reality is an illusion of the false self, in the same way his direction and narration of the radio broadcast of H. G. Wells's novel *The War of the Worlds* created a false panic about a Martian invasion. The very illusion that thrust the twenty-three-year-old Welles into notoriety and stardom. Prominence, celebrity, power, the very places where the false self thrives most.

In fact, as social neuroscience and evolutionary psychology have shown us, we aren't born alone. We are literally born from the body of another. We are born into a community. Even abandoned children like me are often surrounded by a team of medical workers and adopted parents. Our life is dependent on the presence of others to care for us. Left alone, infants die. With no one to provide us with food, shelter, love. And this was a common form of birth control in ancient Rome. Thus, the countercultural activity of the first Christians who recovered the *anairetoi* from the trash heap . . . "the picked-up ones." They nurtured the throwaways in a community of compassion.

No matter how much harm we cause, it's unlikely we will die alone. Even people who don't have "a person" often have a caring nurse. Someone will likely transport our body. Incinerate it or bury it. Someone will likely pronounce "ashes to ashes, dust to dust." And no matter what great lengths we go to live apart from God, to locate ourselves elsewhere from the divine, we will in some way be reunified with God, and reunified with all humans ever, everywhere.

Relationships that sustain our earliest days of life are real. The relationships that make us who we are, clothe us, feed us, teach us skills . . . very much real. Our very consciousness is shaped by our relationships with others in a real way. The bundle of relationship that will send us into our final rest . . . real. The great cloud of withnesses who will nurture us along the way, yep, you guessed it . . . real. Human beings are an unexplainable species outside the context of relationships. We are first and foremost social beings. Our social *real*ity is reality.

We are certainly not born alone, we certainly can't really live alone, and we likely won't die alone. Our "love and friendship" does not create the "illusion for the moment that we're not alone." Our love and friendship are the ultimate reality of our eternal realness.

If we understand Merton's insight into the "oneness we already are," aloneness is a lie. It always has been. We are actually *never alone*. And that's not the panic of an illusionary Martian invasion. That is real. And our spiritual development must be nurtured in the context of real relationships. Our soul formation is also communally determined. Or as John Wesley, founder of Methodism said, "The gospel of Christ knows of no religion, but social; no holiness but social holiness. Faith working by love, is the length and breadth and depth and height of Christian perfection."[12]

I do wonder if our society's undergirding understanding of *real* is more Welles than Merton.

Real virtuality?

Earlier we saw the human tendency to try to create counterfeit community with tools of loneliness in an attempt to live apart from God. Cain settles in the land of Nod, east of Eden where the first city is constructed, instruments and pipes are developed for music, and where they forge the first tools from bronze and iron (Genesis 4:16–22). Noah, on the other hand, uses technology for good purposes, building an ark that sustains human and animal community.

At Babel, the people utilize the new technology of brick-baking and mortar to construct a tower that both seeks to penetrate and supersede the perceived space where God dwells (Genesis 11:4). Not all community is compassionate or real. Humans have been using technology in both harmful and helpful ways since the origin of our existence. Have we used technologies today to create a shallow and inauthentic Babel-like form of community?

Sociologist Manuel Castells describes the network society as a social structure enabled by microelectronics-based information and communications technologies.[13] He suggests that we must now recognize two different kinds of space: the *space of place* and the *space of flows*. Castells believes that space, throughout human history, has been "the material support of simultaneity in social practice." So cities, for instance, are communication systems, increasing the chance of communication through physical contiguity (direct contact). He calls the *space of place* the space of contiguity.[14]

The internet, along with computerized transportation, create the possibility of simultaneity introduced in social relationships at a distance (distanced contact). Meaning, humans no longer need to interact face-to-face in a physical place to have "contact." This transformation of the spatiality of social interaction through simultaneity creates a new kind of space: *the space of flows*. Castells defines the space of flows as "the material support of simultaneous social practices communicated at a distance."[15]

Timothy Luke, building on the work of Castells, shows that cyberspace is an expression of the nodes, hubs, and flows of the network. In other words, the digital space of bits and bytes is the result of the "machinic infrastructure of boxes and wires, cables and satellites, servers and relays that anchor the built networks, which, in turn, generate such new, hyperreal electronic environments." Luke shows that cyberspace is more than mere clusters of code experienced as audio, graphics, text, or video out on the network, but "these digital objects constitute portals into the experience of new types of community, work, identity, sex, utility, knowledge, or power in e-public forms of life."[16]

In short, the network is the machinery that creates the web, enabling a new form of space, and time. It is the infrastructure for what has been called the digital age. So in the same way that cities provided opportunity for encounter in the space of place, the digital ecosystem facilitates distanced contact in the space of flows. A city is a built environment that both facilitates and limits the movement of people through space. The web is similar to a city: it is a digitally built environment that facilitates and limits the movement of people through a virtual ecosystem.

Castells suggests that the web and wireless communications are more than traditional media, they are a global means of interactive, multimodal, mass self-communication. Writing from 2000, Castells recognized that for hundreds of millions of internet users under thirty, online communities have become a fundamental dimension of everyday life that keeps growing everywhere . . . online communities are fast developing not as a virtual world, but as a "real virtuality" integrated with other forms of interaction in an increasingly hybridized everyday life.[17]

How have these prophetic explanations of the emerging social structures held up twenty years later? For digital natives (those born with screens in their homes), social networks, such as Facebook, X, and Instagram, constitute a very real part of life. But do these technologies enable a depth of connection and quality of community?

MIT sociologist Sherry Turkle in *Alone Together* questions the quality of community that can be achieved online.

She writes, "Communities are places where one feels safe enough to take the good and the bad. In communities, others come through for us in hard times, so we are willing to hear what they have to say, even if we don't like it." She reminds us that community literally means "to give among each other."[18]

Turkle began to think of the digital ecosystem as a "third place." Yet she ultimately decided that the convenient nature of fast-friends in cyberspace—friends easily made and easily lost—did not hold up to the classic understanding of community: "Communities are constituted by physical proximity, shared concerns, real consequences, and common responsibilities."[19]

In online environments, it's easy to break off or out of relationships with the touch of a button. Furthermore, the powerful supercomputers we hold in the palm of our hands, and unlimited access to online connectivity, has led to the fraying of the real molecule-swapping relationships right in front of us. Parents are too distracted to be present with children. Spouses escape from the difficult aspects of intimate relationships by retreating online. Employees use work hours to escape the clock, their bodies present in the office but their cognitive presence extended across time and space. In other words, they are not present, and productivity suffers. Turkle describes it this way, "We are forever elsewhere."[20]

I have advocated for a blended ecology of online and on-site forms of church. It is certainly possible to create online community: my team and I planted a church in AltspaceVR for several years. Once a week, people from across the globe would put on our virtual reality headsets and join together in a digitally created space for Living Room Church. As avatars, we would circle up for a time of worship through music, prayer, a sermonic conversation, and yes, even a digital version of holy communion. As the community grew, it began to attract some young digital builders, and they constructed the worlds of biblical scenes. So we would talk about Moses parting the Red Sea, as we walked through the parted waters (complete with Pharaoh's broken chariots and skeletons!) We talked about Jesus healing the man at the pool of Bethesda, as we visited a digital version of the pool itself. Real community was formed there, and real discipleship took place. Throughout the pandemic, when physical church buildings were closed down, this digital community healed our isolation.

We can use our technology to build arks that sustain life, or towers attempting to supersede God and destroy it. However, it is increasingly difficult to balance life between the online and on-site worlds. It is true that we could apply the same critique about "authentic community" to analog congregations, but there are noticeable increases in loneliness in this new hybrid life.[21]

Let's return to the insight from Haidt in *The Anxious Generation*, and the impact of digital technology on youth mental health. The rise in adolescent mental health issues, particularly among Generation Z, are clearly connected to smartphone use, social media, and helicopter parenting restricting unsupervised outdoor play. The shift from play-based to phone-based childhoods has disrupted adolescent development.[22]

Consider the differences between children in the 1970s, running the neighborhood, climbing trees, and eating worms, to children today, who have replaced those activities with virtually mediated experiences on screens.

Haidt's work is grounded in good research. It shows that smartphones are certainly positively correlated with the rise in childhood and adolescent mental health issues. "Soon after teens got iPhones, they started getting more depressed." Haidt argues that play-based childhoods, not phone-based childhoods, promote healthy development. Our health is adversely impacted by sleep deprivation and attention fragmentation associated with smartphone usage. These devices also accelerate polarization and diminish participation in moral communities that give us a sense of meaning and purpose.[23]

However, the negative impacts of smartphones and social media can be curbed. Haidt suggests four important reforms for children and adolescents:

1. No smartphones before high school. Parents should delay entry into the 24/7 internet access world.
2. No social media before sixteen. Children need to progress through the most vulnerable period of brain development before they get connected to a firehose of social comparison and algorithmically chosen influencers.
3. Phone-free schools. All schools elementary through high school should mandate students to store smart devices in lockers until the end of the day.
4. Far more unsupervised play and childhood independence. It's through play that children naturally develop social skills, overcome anxiety, and become self-governing young adults.[24]

It seems that our technologies are leading us more towards Nod and Babel than building Noah's ark. The powerful devices that we use every day are rapidly rewiring consciousness and human relationships like nothing before in human history. This is negatively impacting our ability to think, focus, and be attentive to others. By bending us towards self-fixation, it is decreasing our capacity for compassion and prosocial behaviors, limiting our ability to build close relationships. For example, studies have noted the overall decrease in compassion among US undergraduates between 1979 and 2009. In general, our society has been trending downward in empathetic concern for others and civic orientation.[25]

Real healing

There is a myth that we are wounded as an individual, then go on a heroic journey of healing as an individual. Many modern therapeutic modalities are undergirded by this logic. But this is a dangerous and deceptive idea.

We are created for community. We are wounded in community. We are healed in community. In *Painting with Ashes*, I suggested that compassion-centered expressions of church are needed in the fallout of a society in which a leading cause of disaffiliation from churches is the harmful ideas and behaviors of Christians. Compassion-centered communities give people space to articulate these experiences and thus have three essential ingredients. They need to be *accessible*, *safe*, and *real*.

- *Accessible*: These communities form in normal spaces where people gather and speak in the common vernacular of the people. The only requirement to participate is a hunger for connection and belonging.
- *Safe*: The communities meet in smaller, intimate groups. All people from every social status are welcome, and harmful behaviors are not tolerated.
- *Real*: People are invited to come to terms with and express their wounds. We ask, "How goes it with your soul?" People are free to name their spiritual progress and roadblocks in a community of reciprocity and mutual support.[26]

Early church communities were places of embodied healing that were *accessible*, *safe*, and *real*. The three-part *Never Alone* framework offers a way of "salvation" which flows from a vision of holistic healing that takes place in community. It is a journey of healing and unification that begins in this life and continues in the next. This starts from the utter conviction of the goodness of humanity, but also holds in tension our current experience of loneliness.

Often, we can point to some trauma that occurred at the hands of an individual or group. We can identify that trauma and how it affected us. If we can find the source of our pain, we can begin to heal from it. Typically, in the Anglosphere nations, a compensated professional guides us through that journey. The goal is to heal the ego wound, reintegrate, and self-actualize.

In the meantime, we can nurture the poison of resentment in our souls. Harboring unforgiveness, living in a cycle of toxic shame and blame.

According to researchers Ardelt and Sharma, the hallmarks of wisdom are the ability to take the long view, to see the bigger picture, to think systemically, and to be comfortable with paradoxes. Their research on organizational wisdom reveals that wise leaders have self-reflective and interpersonal skills in addition to knowledge and cognitive skills. Wise leaders strive to make good judgments that promote the success of all the people in a system. "We are all in this together" is the attitude of wise leaders, who are primarily motivated by supporting others, uniting people, and seeking overall human flourishing.[27]

Hurt people hurt people. Wounded harmers are often acting out of the patterns of harm they themselves received.

Consider substance abuse disorder, mentioned earlier. Addiction, the disease of isolation. It's a death spiral. We use to isolate. We are isolated in a state of self-fixation while using even when surrounded by others. We die of loneliness. Community is the cure for the disease. And community is hard. Perhaps twelve-step fellowships understand the biblical origins of *koinonia* in deeper ways than churches do at times. Because we know our very lives depend on leaning in to the community, even when it's hard.

One tool of the twelve-step process is a searching and fearless moral inventory. First, we look at all of our resentments. Who harmed us? What was the cause? What did it affect throughout our lives? This might be our sex relations, self-esteem, and finances. Where did we have fears, imagined and actual? This work encapsulates the first three columns of our inventory.

But there is a fourth column . . . what was our part? What role did we play in the development of these resentments? What did we do with these wounds? How did we wound others? Any time we have a finger pointing out toward someone else, three are pointing back at us. When we notice the speck in our neighbor's eye, there is always a plank protruding from our own (Matthew 7:3). The movement into true self is the movement into non-judgment.

There is profound alignment between the wisdom of the twelve steps and the work of the Arbinger Institute around conflict resolution in *The Anatomy of Peace*. In life, and especially during conflict, we either have "a heart at peace" or "a heart at war."[28]

When our heart is at peace, we are aware where we stand, but we remain open to explore other sides and possibilities. We lead with wonder, curiosity, open-mindedness, and humility.

We can rest in the reality that our "struggle is not against flesh and blood" (Ephesians 6:12), meaning other humans.

We view those who disagree with us as beloved children of God, fearfully and wonderfully made, part of the divine unity that's already there, and we treat them accordingly. We disarm our other by disarming ourselves.

Conversely, a heart at war sees the other as enemy. We are closed off to standing-under to *under*stand by the rigidity of our own position and assumptions. We cannot even entertain a perceived compromise, so we gear up to protect, divide, and conquer. In this state we are on high alert, and often restless, irritable, and discontent. We baptize our position with divine right and aggressively enforce our beliefs, even if it harms others. People become objects and obstacles that we blame, dismiss, or ignore. These are the weapons of the false self.

When we have a heart at war, we tear at the fabric of the "oneness we already are" described by Merton. We cannot be in a true place of unity and community with others in this state.

A heart at war has strong correlations with the attitude Jesus confronted in the religious leaders. As we saw earlier, they seemed to have certain ideas around how their ancestry and their interpretation of God's law placed them in an elite and superior class (Matthew 3:7–9; Mark 10:5). Jesus called them "blind guides" (Matthew 15:14; 23:16, 24). Their eye condition was connected to a deadly heart condition, which he described as *pōrōsis* (hardened) *kardia*: (heart) (Mark 3:5 NRSVue). In several of those encounters, Jesus highlighted their diminished way of seeing others, their lack of empathy, their stubborn resistance to live in solidarity with those experiencing suffering.

We are not responsible for the wounds we have suffered, but we are responsible for our healing.

Purging the poison

As people who are created to love, our healing involves relationships with others. When humanity experienced that original trauma, one of the major breaks was not just in our relationship with God, but our relationship with each other.

We are hiding in the garden, "naked and afraid," not just separated from God but from one another (Genesis 3). In Christ, we are reconciled in all those fragmented relationships, and commissioned to be instruments of reconciliation (2 Corinthians 5:18). We can be in the kind of relationships with one another that God intended from the beginning.

Most of us are limping from wounds in this department. Chances are high that at some point in our life someone we loved, someone we opened ourselves to in a vulnerable way, disappointed or even harmed us. Sometimes this wounding comes from the very familial figures who were supposed to protect us from that kind of harm. Those wounds can become a source of shame and pain that many may carry their entire lives. They can diminish our capacity to love ourselves and others.

Holding on to resentments can be likened to "drinking poison and expecting the other party to die." Resentment doesn't hurt them, it only hurts us. Resentment is a kind of mechanism to "re-feel" something. It imprisons us in a memory of harm. We maintain a negative sentiment, reliving and nurturing it again and again over time. When we are trapped in our own agony of isolation, fear, and resentment, we act out our brokenness and bring harm to others.

Yet in Christ there is healing from those wounds. The key to this healing is *forgiveness*. Forgiveness is not forgetting. It's not excusing the harm done to us. It's a spiritual process through which we can let go of our anger, sadness, disappointment, and frustration. Forgiveness is the only pathway to peace. Simple but not easy.

This is an essential aspect of Jesus' teaching, and in fact, it's located right in the center of the Lord's Prayer. "And forgive us our debts, as we also have forgiven our debtors" (Matthew 6:12). Jesus goes on to interpret what he means by this, saying "For if you forgive others their trespasses, your heavenly Father will also forgive you" (Matthew 6:14 NRSVue).

In recovery fellowships we have a practical way to live out Jesus' instructions. If we realize we are carrying a resentment against someone, we pray for that person (literally as Jesus tells us to pray for our enemies, Matthew 5:44). We pray for them every day for a minimum of two weeks (sometimes longer). We pray for God to bless them, to pour out provision and healing for them, to give them health, happiness, and prosperity. We pray every day until we mean it. Whether or not that person changes, the prayer process always changes us.

It's possible that in our woundedness we hurt other people. We have in some way damaged the social fabric of the tapestry of oneness. If we are carrying guilt about harm we have caused, this phase of our journey towards the real self involves going back to make amends. We can't just say, "Hey, I'm a Christian, sorry to everyone I ever hurt out there, but I'm all better now!" We must go and make things right with those we have hurt. I remember sitting down with my own sponsor seventeen years ago to create my amends list. It included every person I had wronged and every financial debt I owed . . . a whole notebook full! But one by one, my sponsor guided me through that process of making those amends.

Jesus tells a story about this. He says, "So when you are offering your gift at the altar, if you remember that your brother or sister has something against you, leave your gift

there before the altar and go; first be reconciled to your
brother or sister, and then come and offer your gift" (Matthew
5:23–24 NRSVue).

To me, this communicates that restored relationships with
our fellow human siblings are more important than religious
rituals and offering sacrifices. Wouldn't it be great if simply
making an offering could heal wounds between people? However, it does not. We must actually go and offer the necessary
actions and words that heal the wounds of those we've harmed.

It might become obvious that this is not something that
has been widely practiced in the modern church. Over decades
of pastoral counseling and church planting I've heard many
people express wounds that they have been nurturing for a
lifetime. Because the Christian faith has been reduced to an
intellectual endeavor, accepting a set of propositions, there is no
implicit assumption that we are actually to do all the things
Jesus teaches us to do. Because the practice of our faith has
been so individualistic, with little regard for the collectivistic
dimension, we have a collapsed view of community. If we attend church services, give offerings, and serve on committees,
we are doing our part to uphold our institutional membership
vows. We have a "church" that we belong to.

This is a sad parody of knowing and following Jesus. We
end up living a diminished life, not the life that is abundant.
To use Jesus' own words, "The thief comes only to steal and
kill and destroy. I came that they may have life and have it
abundantly" (John 10:10 NRSVue). In this case the thief is an
institutional iteration of the church that ignores the profound
emphasis that Jesus places on relationships.

There is no freedom in the world like knowing we have
done our best to repair the damage we have caused. The ability to live without looking over our shoulders. A soul in which

the God-given alarm system of guilt has been silenced, and loneliness cured through community.

Perhaps the hardest part of Jesus' teaching comes here, "A new command I give you: Love one another. As I have loved you, so you must love one another" (John 13:34). Whoa, Jesus! That is setting the bar really high! The community of disciples is to love one another the way Jesus loves us. And to go further, it's through this love the world knows "you are my disciples" (John 13:35). It is actually through embodying the original unity that the church becomes a sign, instrument, and foretaste of God's peaceable kingdom breaking into the world.

In the community of disciples, how we love one another is the witness to the world that we are the body of Christ. But it's not just our relationships with those in the church through which we must embody this love. We need to ask, "Who is my neighbor?" in this "love thy neighbor" command. The answer is that every single human being we will ever meet is our neighbor.

Again, Jesus came healing Gentiles, commending the faith of centurions (the symbol of Roman oppression over a subjugated people), eating with tax collectors, siding with condemned adulterers, and telling crazy stories about "good Samaritans." Jesus expands the concept of neighbor back to the original intent of God blessing all the tribes of the earth through Abraham (Genesis 12:3) and the prophetic glimpses of a messiah through whom all people would be brought into a peaceable kingdom (Isaiah 2, 11), and a day when all the Gentiles would stream to the light of YHWH through Israel (Isaiah 60:3).

This is where Micah 6:8 has a relevant word for us, "He has told you, O mortal, what is good and what does the LORD require of you but to do justice and to love kindness and to walk humbly with your God?" (NRSVue).

Doing justice also includes giving of ourselves in sacrificial ways for the sake of others. It includes costly action on our part, to become "repairers of the breach" who speak and act to bring healing in the midst of oppression (Isaiah 58:12).

It includes us doing what Jesus calls of us in Matthew 25:31–46, to feed the hungry, provide drink for the thirsty, invite and shelter strangers, clothe the naked, care for the sick, and visit those in prison. In fact, in doing these things for others, we are doing them for the Jesus who indwells them. This is a spirituality of compassion.

The real power of confession

In the twelve-step recovery fellowships, we have another cliché. It is the crystallized spiritual wisdom of millions of recovering people: "We are only as sick as our secrets."

The fourth step inventory asks us to write all of those secrets down on paper, and then in the fifth step, we confess them out loud to God, ourselves, and another human being. Later, we go back and make amends "wherever possible" to all the people we have harmed.

It is often in this place of honest confession that so many falter along the spiritual path of healing. In Jesus' miracles, confession and forgiveness of sin are often connected with healing.

James 5:16 tells us, "Confess your sins to one another and pray for one another, so that you may be healed" (NRSVue), but rarely do Christians grapple with the power of this truth.

Is it possible to have our sins forgiven and yet not be healed? Are those one and the same phenomenon?

Catholics have long known the healing power of confession, one of their seven sacraments. But this is often lost among Protestant Christians. Protestants argue that we don't need a "middleman" to get to God. Through Jesus' death on the cross, which tore the temple veil in two, all humans now have equal access to God. Through Christ's wounded body, we can pass into the temple's Most Holy Place (or, Holy of Holies). We can confess our sin directly to God and receive forgiveness.

Yet if we take James 5 seriously, confession that leads to healing requires "one another." The sin that lies hidden in our hearts rots our souls from the inside out. That toxic guilt and shame trapped in our bodies can cause physical and mental illness. The emotional pain of loneliness which flows from a state of isolation keeps us trapped in the death spiral. Yet when we can confess those things to God and another human, healing takes place.

Recovery and healing from our woundedness are bound up with the honest confession of our sin to at least one other person. We don't need to tell *everyone* about our sin, but we need to tell *someone* about it, someone we can trust. Also, this is not a one-time event, it is a lifelong journey.

The importance of this part of our spiritual healing cannot be understated. Many lifelong church attendees never truly find healing because they miss this communal aspect. Without the experiencing of release provided through confession, we hold on to the darkest of human emotions, including resentment, fear, pride, lust, racism, sexism, and judgment. The fruits of the Spirit cannot grow in a heart still crowded with these roots of bitterness. Being able to truly experience love, joy, peace, patience, kindness, goodness, faithfulness, gentleness, and self-control requires a heart soil that has been cleansed from the weeds of secret sin.

True healing takes place within the cradle of safe relationships.

Confession in the safety of a trusting relationship is a healing balm. This is part of the magic that I believe happens in twelve-step meetings. The biblical principle of confession takes place in groups like these at times when people are fully honest with themselves and with one another. These are places where we can just be real, talk about struggles, and get them out of our heads. We all need to use our stories in ways that will bring healing to others who carry the same wounds. This is one reason I hope that we discover *all people* are in recovery. We are all in some way on a healing journey from the original trauma.

In the space of confession, we acknowledge our brokenness and pain. We learn about a God of unconditional love and then *commune* with that God—maybe for the first time.

From an Afrocentric perspective this is communal healing. I mentioned how in Western schools of therapy, the highly trained and well compensated expert guides the client toward individuation, self-realization, and a well-developed ego. However, African therapeutic modalities include testimony therapy, which focuses on sharing in a collective story. Testimony therapy is communitarian and social constructionist in nature. Ubuntu—if we are persons through other persons our healing will most powerfully manifest in community with others.

This is a group therapeutic process that brings healing to individuals in the context of community. It is a resource for marginalized and oppressed people who are denied access to some of the more exclusive (and expensive) Western healing modalities employed by individualistic cultures. Communal healing of individual and collective trauma is closely aligned with the collectivistic culture of the Hebrew people and the tradition of lament.[29]

At one of our churches in Florida, we are three congrega-tions, one church. Wildwood UMC partners with God's Glory Ministries, a Black church plant, and Iglesia Gosen, a Hispanic congregation, both of which are in the Pentecostal tradition. We share space, life, and ministry, and collaboratively lead a dinner church together called Taste of Grace. A dinner church is simply a worship experience centered around a communal meal. Each week someone shares a personal testimony or Jesus story. Sometimes those testimonies include personal struggles, and deep lament, but as a community we rally around the storyteller in a collective embrace of healing.

If communal life in Jesus is the one unique gift that can heal a world experiencing an epidemic of loneliness and isolation, the most urgent, compassionate, and restorative thing we can possibly do is cultivate new forms of church with people who don't go to church. These contextual churches like Taste of Grace, Burritos and Bibles, Tattoo Parlor Church, Shenani-gans, and Higher Power Hour are little real communities where the four healing questions from testimony therapy are our guide:

1. What happened to you?
2. How does what happened to you affect you now?
3. What do you need to heal?
4. In spite of what happened to you, what gives you strength to go on?

Real healing requires vulnerability in an atmosphere of grace.

People need a safe community where they can take the bandages off their wounds. The healing process requires us to appropriately grieve our losses and come to terms with our trauma. This necessitates us being real . . . articulating our grieving in an uncensored way. This is why many people report that twelve-step fellowships are more transformative than church communities. Recovery meetings provide perhaps the clearest example of testimony therapy . . . and it only costs one dollar in the basket.

The book of Psalms is a powerful resource to assist us in our healing. It facilitates us through Brueggemann's threefold schematic for our common human experience in transit along the flow of orientation, disorientation, reorientation. The psalmists provide us an entire collection of poem-like prayers, called laments, to help us journey through disorientation. A lament gives us a vehicle to release the toxic infection of our wounds. Laments can also help us discover the truth of King David's admission to God: "If I make my bed in the depths, you are there" (Psalm 139:8). Pain is real, and yet God is somehow there with us in the midst of it. These are psalms in which honest anguish, deep distress, and heart-cry despair can be shared in community with others. Healing begins when we articulate these emotions in an uncensored way.

When we unveil our wounds with others, God does God's best work through us. This doesn't mean we go around spewing our pain upon others. Pain, trauma, and loss require an appropriate process of grieving. Untreated wounds keep us sick. But paradoxically, God uses wounded healers to heal other wounded people.

Real healing is unleashed in a communal atmosphere of compassion where people are free to be vulnerable.

We live in a world that is wounded and weeping. Our pace rarely gives space to grieve and get real. But there is a wounded healer who longs to hold us in our tears. Healing takes place in safe conditions where honest stories of woundedness can be shared. These communities provide holding space where people can process their trauma in an unfiltered way.

As we gather in that circle in a tattoo parlor and share our stories, we are doing in a modern way what the psalmist was doing in the lament psalms. Sometimes the anger is aimed at God, and that's okay. We can beat our fists on God's chest until we can't lift our arms anymore. God can take it! We can lie on God's lap and cry ourselves to sleep; God will be there when we wake up. This kind of healing takes place most powerfully in community.

A church always singing doxology, a liturgical formula of celebratory praise to God, and never lament, is not being real. Loss and pain require an appropriate period of grieving. A church that never gives space for this will be unhealthy. We are inadvertently minimizing people's loss and grief, diminishing their capacity to heal.

The psalms teach us how to *get real*. Lament psalms are a resource for communal healing. They give us a vehicle to articulate our emotions to God in an honest way.

My God, my God, why have you forsaken me?
    Why are you so far from saving me,
    so far from my cries of anguish?
My God, I cry out by day, but you do not answer,
    by night, but I find no rest." (Psalm 22:1–2)

In your unfailing love, silence my enemies;
    destroy all my foes,
    for I am your servant. (Psalm 143:12)

Blessed is he who seizes your infants
    and dashes them against the rocks. (Psalm 137:9 BSB)

The language of lament is not neat and clean. It is raw, primitive, and real. It is an honest expression of the language of grief. If we hold on to these emotions, they keep us sick and stuck. Real community gives people space to express their struggles and find real healing. They can expose the distortions of the false self and help us find original unity.

Emerging generations are rarely finding congregations that embody this kind of community, and for the vast majority church has simply become inaccessible. Many people will never walk into our sanctuary on Sunday mornings no matter how amazing worship might be. So we must form these healing communities in the spaces and rhythms where people do life, around the practices that already connect them there. They become like little islands of togetherness in a tempest-tossed sea of raging isolation.

Cultivating these healing communities, where people can be made *whole*, can help heal a holey world. In the next chapter, I want to provide a framework that can show you how.

6

Whole Communities

*The Spirit told me to go with them and not
to make a distinction between them and us.*

—ACTS 11:12 NRSVue

Can church be *good* to someone like my friend Tracy who experienced it as mostly *bad*? Can we cultivate communities that don't abandon people like Olive in the final weeks of her life? Can people like my little brother McKinley find a community that might touch their soul in a deep way, halting them to rethink jamming a needle in their arm?

Is there really a whole gospel, for the whole world? How can we embody good news with people for whom it is not only *good* but *news*? Or are we content to keep sharing the same news with the same people, week after week? What does this good news have to say to a society experiencing an epidemic of loneliness and isolation?

If we are going to cultivate whole communities, that make people whole, we need to consider that we are on the edge of a new Pentecost, an outpouring of the Holy Spirit that might heal our polarized, traumatized, and lonely world. It might look something like what happens in Cornelius's house, when Peter gets dragged by the Spirit into what is arguably one of the most profound revelations in the New Testament in Acts chapter 10.

At this point, the church has been a movement primarily among Jewish believers. Most of the action has been centered in Jerusalem. A fledgling church is seeking to do life "together" and holding "all things in common; they would sell their possessions and goods and distribute the proceeds to all, as any had need. Day by day, as they spent much time together in the temple, they broke bread at home and ate their food with glad and generous hearts, praising God and having the goodwill of all the people. And day by day the Lord added to their number those who were being saved" (Acts 2:44–47 NRSVue).

Here is a portrait of the holistic ecology of church. They make sure everyone is cared for. There is a true sense of community and togetherness. They don't just go to temple, but also break bread in homes daily. Today we would describe this as emerging and inherited forms of church living together in symbiotic relationship, a blended ecology. Outsiders are regularly coming into the community. The church is flourishing on the edge, with a commitment to the center.

However, in Acts 10, the circle expands. The edge moves further out to the periphery. It starts in Caesarea where there was a man named Cornelius, a "centurion of the Italian Cohort, as it was called" (NRSVue). Cornelius has a vision in which an angel instructs him to invite a stranger named Peter to his home. The same day, Peter has a vision of a big picnic blanket lowered from the heavens filled with unclean animals and a voice that says, "Take and feast." Peter, in his typical Petrine pattern of threefold resistance, repeats: "No unclean thing has touched my lips." But the voice of the Lord says, "What God has made clean, you must not call profane" (Acts 10:15 NRSVue). Whoa, this is big!

The ecstatic vision was the Holy Spirit setting Peter up to go have church at Cornelius's house. Cornelius, an "unclean" Gentile, Roman centurion. When Peter arrives at Cornelius's home, Cornelius shares about his vision. Peter begins to preach about Jesus. Shockingly, the Spirit is poured out on Cornelius and all his household, just as it had been in Jerusalem. They begin to speak in tongues. Peter, the reluctant apostle to Gentiles begins to baptize this new Christian community. Together. Diversity. Togetheversity. The church expands in a fresh way that even Peter had yet to envision (Acts 10:44–48).

Next Peter goes back to the church in Jerusalem to share the story of Pentecost, the sequel. As he shared this story with other Jerusalem church leaders, he describes the specifics of the Spirit's instructions, "The Spirit told me to go with them and not to make a distinction between them and us" (Acts 11:12 NRSVue). Can you hear in this sentence the wisdom of compassion that understands every human interaction from the foundation of solidarity? Can you hear Merton's pure grace of "infused contemplation" and the awakening to the "oneness that's already there"? The Jerusalem church celebrates together, "Then God has given even to the gentiles the repentance that leads to life" (Acts 11:18 NRSVue). This is a vision of life as ever-widening circles of wholeness.

Perhaps movements like Fresh Expressions are bringing us to another Pentecost-at-Cornelius's-house moment? So how do we practically cultivate these whole communities of togetherness?

Seven generations

Native American wisdom is collectivistic. For thousands of years, the Indigenous peoples who have inhabited the

American continents thought about creation and community in terms of the interrelatedness of all things. The Sacred Circle of Life describes an intense and deep connectedness with Mother Earth, personal relationships, family, neighborhoods, communities, nations, plant beings, four-legged siblings, the finned and flying beings, and the Great Spirit that animates all the universe contains. In the Sacred Circle, human beings can and must live in union with one another and the land.

One healing concept bequeathed to the human family through Native wisdom is the Seventh Generation Principle. It is based on an ancient Haudenosaunee (Iroquois) philosophy that the decisions we make today should result in a sustainable world seven generations into the future. This idea originated from the Great Law of the Haudenosaunee, the founding document of the Iroquois Confederacy. The principle is generally referred to regarding decisions about energy, water, and natural resources, and ensuring those decisions are sustainable for seven generations into the future, "the people downstream from us, whose faces we will never see."[1]

Seven generations is about the length of time people often have the capacity to imagine, but if we are honest, how many of us think beyond ourselves, or our children, and grandchildren?

Any conversation about cultivating communities of wholeness must include as many diverse voices and perspectives as possible. If we take the possibility of oneness and unification seriously, we will need to build a bigger table. This is why I believe compassion to be such a holistic and unifying concept. It is foundational to every world religion, and it is a value, to some degree, of every culture. Perhaps it is a divine thread of the innate goodness that is already there. The table must also include the spectrum of generations. We cannot discard the sage wisdom of the seniors in the tribe, bowing at the altar of youthfulness, nor can we silence young voices at the table.

Earlier we glimpsed at the research of Monika Ardelt on forms of religiosity and the impact on well-being with the chronologically mature. What do we know of the spirituality of the young? If we are going to think generatively, one place to start is with the Springtide Research Institute, which focuses on understanding the values and experiences among young people aged 13 to 25. This research explores how emerging generations make sense of our rapidly evolving social system. According to Springtide survey data, the hallmarks of engaging young people will be *curiosity, wholeness, connection,* and *flexibility.*[2]

Sadly, none of these four concepts are prominent features of inherited church systems. We are known as the answer-having people, not the question-asking, curiosity people. We are known to emphasize a post-mortem idea of salvation, focused on eternal destiny, rather than healing and communal wholeness in this life. We are known to be a people of superficial connections, propositional and performative religion, who do religious programs then go back to "real" life. So many branches of the denominational and nondenominational tree are known to be rigid, inflexible, and fixed in our ways. It's as if we are unfamiliar with the forgotten beatitude of Jesus: "Blessed are the *flexible* for they shall not get bent out of shape."

The State of Religion and Young People 2023 reports massive spiritual openness among young people, but deep skepticism about the trustworthiness of religious institutions and their leaders. They found some key discoveries about the spirituality of the young:

1. *Sacred experiences beyond worship spaces*: While young people may not find sacred experiences in traditional places of worship, they are indeed seeking the sacred. Their inner lives are complex, and they desire meaningful encounters.
2. *Cultivating sacred sensibility*: Young people are cultivating a "sacred sensibility" through connection, relationships, and community. For them, the sacred is about connecting with others.
3. *Building spaces for connection*: To engage young people, leaders should focus on building spaces where connection thrives—spaces that foster belonging and allow for sacred encounters.[3]

Another of Springtide's key findings was the identification of eight core values that drive America's young adults: accountable, inclusive, authentic, welcoming, impactful, relational, growthful, and meaningful. Sadly, these are values often not associated with inherited congregations.

Here's the exciting news. Jesus was about cultivating sacred experiences beyond formal religious spaces; he formed his disciples to cultivate sacred sensibility; he went about building spaces for relational connection. His life and teaching were oriented away from his own desires, and conscious of the generations who had come before and would come later (Matthew 8:11). Matthew and Luke carefully document the genealogy of Jesus, tracing his connection back to the first elders. Jesus instructed the community that would bear his name to do "greater things" than he was doing (John 14:12). He prepared generations of followers to be on the lookout for the Great Spirit, who would "guide [them] into all the truth" (John 16:13–15).

Can we cultivate faith communities now with seven generations in mind? What does sustainability look like amid a crumbling Christendom, in which financial models, leadership formation, space usage, and structural hierarchies are being found to be unsustainable?

Fresh expressions of church

Throughout this book I have referenced small, agile faith communities gathering in the everyday spaces and rhythms of life. Compassion-centered communities that are good, real, and whole. These communities we are cultivating on the ground are part of a global movement called Fresh Expressions of Church.

These are communities like Ka:ll, led by my friend Rev. Danielle Buwon Kim in Dallas, Texas, who gathers people around the table to "enjoy Asian food together, expose and heal Asian Americans and Pacific Islanders (AAPI) invisibility created by the model minority myth, and reclaim our Christian faith to liberate and re-create a world that looks more like the kin-dom of God."[4] They look like Creciendo Juntas (Growing Together), an artistic community of belonging for Hispanic/Latino and Anglo women led by Jaidymar Smith in her small town of Ramseur, North Carolina.[5] Or these can be online hybrid communities like The Well, led by Pastor Rai Jackson, in Washington, DC, a creative arts and conscious awareness faith community that "embraces the arts, navigates purpose and evokes healthy conversation around spirituality, justice, and Jesus."[6]

The movement began in the United Kingdom, where the decline of the church and erosion of Christendom is decades ahead of the United States. While massive historic spaces are sparsely populated on Sunday mornings, thousands of these fresh expressions are emerging just beyond the stained glass cathedrals. People with no connection to any church are gathering in these new forms of church.

The movement, while simmering below the surface for some time, was unleashed in 2004 with the creation of the *Mission-Shaped Church* report. The working party led by Bishop Graham Cray was the first to identify these new communities as "Fresh Expressions" in alignment with the Anglican Declaration of Assent, "to proclaim the gospel afresh in every generation."[7]

The movement very quickly became global in nature, with some version of Fresh Expressions emerging on every continent. Most of us who were early practitioners seemed to have been intuitively following the Spirit in the cultivation of these communities. For years Jill and I were failing-forward, empowering laity to start a recovery church, and faith communities in a rural barbecue diner, a tattoo parlor, and a burrito joint. People began to alert us that what we were doing was called Fresh Expressions. Once we heard there were other people doing similar things, we were relieved to learn we weren't the only crazy ones! We began to connect up and form new networks, curating best practices, and developing a kind of wisdom bank.

Soon I found myself being requested to come and work with churches and leaders, training them how to start these communities. Now our team leads around one hundred on-site and online trainings every year. I have created a Fresh Expressions house of studies, and offer courses at several seminaries, including Duke, Emory, and United.

The movement is connecting with many people who will likely never darken the door of an inherited worship Sunday service. These are people who have never had any previous experience with a faith community, or they are people who have been harmed by Christians and are averse to anything connected to the institutional church. The people who find a spiritual home in these communities span the full spectrum of age, from assisted care facilities, to middle-aged mom groups, to messy churches designed primarily for children and young families.

One of the values of the movement is to be contextual. So the communities start with sensitivity to the context, and nurture relationships organically in an appropriate way. They are also primarily lay-led, meaning everyday Christians are empowered to lead these communities, not just ordained folks. We see a strong sense of ownership and spiritual growth in these expressions of church. They are not your typical spectator sport variety of Christianity. Each person shares in the growth and development of the community as a whole.

Consider my friend Denise. She is a young registered nurse in the radiology department of a local medical center. Her passion is running. She often goes on road trips with her friends to do marathons and mud runs. A friend invited her to a fresh expression that centers around burritos and all-you-can-eat chips and salsa called Burritos and Bibles. She got connected into the community in a deep way and started coming every week. Denise began reading the Bible for the first time and always dropped the most amazing and honest questions into the group.

One time, to close out the gathering, she offered to pray. It was the first time she had ever prayed like this openly in front of a group of people. It was a powerful, unfiltered, and beautiful prayer. She enjoyed offering it and felt ready to take a next step in whatever that would look like. So she jumped into the group text message of our leadership team where we send encouragement, devotional thoughts, and prayer support.

Within six months of her first public prayer, Denise had an idea for her own fresh expression. One line of questioning we often ask our team: What is something you already do every week, where do you do that, who do you do it with? Might that take on a deeper level of spiritual meaning for the people involved? Our lives are already too busy to be adding more stuff. Just keeping up with our normal responsibilities and engaging in spiritual practices in an intentional way can be a lot.

Denise had an aha moment when she thought about all her running buddies. They already have a deep level of relationship. They already get together to engage in a practice they all love. Running already has a deeply spiritual component for some of us who enjoy it. What could happen if they added a couple more explicitly spiritual components? Church 3.1 was born!

Denise and our small team talked about what the group could look like, and what would happen at the gathering. We created a Facebook page and put the group out on different socials. Denise started checking with friends when would be the best time to do a weekly run together, where would be the best place to meet.

In the first gathering, about a dozen people showed up. Denise opened in prayer and said, "If anybody wants to stay after the run, we are just going to have a conversation about helpful spiritual practices." Surprisingly everyone stayed, drying off with towels, hydrating, and doing some cool-down stretches. The community quickly began to have deep spiritual conversations about the mountains and valleys of life. People started to request prayer for different needs in their life. A breakup. A big upcoming job interview. Prayers for patience so "I don't go Old Testament on one of my teenagers!"

Weeks down the road, Denise introduced the Jesus story. Everybody in the group agreed that Jesus was a great teacher. Some in the group weren't so sure he was God. But it didn't really matter what our perspectives were on that, we all had an equal voice.

Denise would simply take out her phone before the run, read a short story about something Jesus said or did, reflected on why it mattered to her, then asked a simple question like, "I love that Jesus said this, what are your thoughts?" or "This story really bugs me and I have lot of questions, what do you all think?" "This running metaphor is really cool, what does pressing on toward the goal spiritually look like for you?" and "If this happened today, what do you think it would look like?"

Now, Denise, a Christian for six months, with no formal theological education or seminary training, is leading a sermonic conversation. It's not a monologue that she carefully crafts in advance, as that would be contextually inappropriate. She just reads a passage, tells a story, asks nonthreatening questions, and leads a dialogue.

Sometimes the conversation time goes on so long it starts to get dark, so we will run, get back, and pick up the conversation. Some people don't engage much in the conversation, some never, but they stay, listen, and slowly open up.

Church 3.1 features prayer, engagement with Scripture, and sometimes confession. We even have sacraments . . . Gatorade (certainly sacramental in University of Florida lands), peanut butter, bananas, and protein bars. We give thanks to the God who imbued us with the ability to run. We have a worshipful moment of community in the wonders of the many Florida green spaces and trails.

This is church. You might say, well where's the pews, hymnals, singing, organ, and _____, fill in the blank. But for the people who are participating in this community, this is their church. They are gathering around the Risen Jesus, finding a whole community, where they can be healed of their loneliness. Where they can be known and loved. Reconnecting with the original unity.

Imagine if every follower of Jesus started one small community like this in some corner of their life. Imagine the impact that would have amid a world where social connections are coming apart. What could a hundred communities like this do to an epidemic of loneliness and isolation? What about a thousand? Or a million. This is the new Pentecost that is taking place right now, all over the world. Here's how we typically go about forming these communities.

The loving first journey

In Fresh Expressions we follow the "loving first journey." It is a way to affirm the good that is already there. Think of it as a journey that takes us through the three motions of the gospel . . . good, alone, together. Let's revisit the three overarching theological movements of Christian spirituality where we started: *original goodness, original trauma, original unity.*

Original goodness—Through *listening* and *loving*, these communities awaken us to our belovedness, the goodness we already are. The U-turn journey begins with stopping, realizing we have been traveling in the wrong direction.

Original trauma—Through *building relationships, forming community*, and exploring *spiritual practices* (or *sharing Jesus*) we move upward into union with Trinity and true self. We begin to heal the traumatic social condition of isolation and the emotional alarm system of loneliness. It continues the U-turn of the first movement by now heading in a new direction, towards God and community.

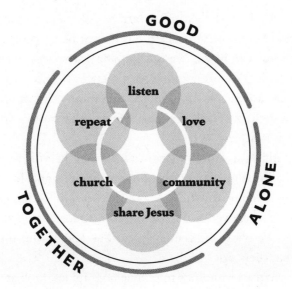

Original unity—Through *becoming church* and *multiplying* little pockets of communal life in Jesus in every nook and cranny of life, we continue the movement outward into communion with neighbor and all life. We discover *koinonia*, the oneness we already are, and we share the eucharistic gift of community with others.

Let me now explain practically what each of the six movements of this "U-turn" journey look like.

Listen—Seeking the good that's already there

We start with listening to God and our community. Think of it as a treasure hunt for the goodness that is already there. We are seeking the goodness that is baked into every place and every person that make up our community.

Like the first disciples we go out two by two, looking for "persons of peace." We are prayerfully listening to how God is already at work before we arrive. We never assume we bring God with us. Our posture is one of being good guests. We are not the hosts. We are looking for spaces where we might gather. We are looking for practices that connect people. What are people up to in our community? What are they doing together? Where are they eating? What stories are they telling themselves?

Sometimes a short prayer walk can be helpful to get us started. We simply pray for different people and locations. Noticing. Paying attention. Making observations. If someone strikes up a conversation, we try to do more listening than talking. We try to be genuinely curious about who they are and what their story is.

We can use technology to pull demographics, look at maps, read reviews of different establishments. Who are the people who live here? What are their socioeconomic realities? What are people saying about the places the Spirit might be leading us to spend time in? Nobody shows up for tattoo church a second time if they get a low-quality tattoo. Burritos and Bibles is no fun if the food isn't good.

Using these tools to understand a community from outside is helpful, but there is no replacement for learning a community from the inside. Spending time incarnationally in the places and with the people the Spirit is drawing us toward. Looking for the life-affirming tendencies and practices that are already there.

Love—Noticing and healing the loneliness in ourselves and others

As we are out in the communities, learning, making connections, we lead with love. How do we genuinely be attentive to the people in this community? Who is flourishing? Who is isolated? Who is unseen? Here we must also become attentive to the *not good*. It is not good that humans should bowl alone. Where can we see and feel the loneliness that we know is there, sometimes hidden beneath the surface?

Where is our gut stirred with love? Why are we feeling that? Is our tendency to move away from painful aspects of our community? Can we stay with it? Turn to sense-making. Ask ourselves how we can be helpful and not harmful.

Where is love already pulsating all over the community? Is it between parents watching their kids play soccer? Is it in the dog lovers who gather at the park for their fur babies to play? Is it in the fitness groups who gather together to prioritize stewardship of the body? Is it at the local pub where the regulars circle up to process another day at their 9–5?

Are there obvious injustices in the community? Hungry children in a food desert. People caught in the grips of addiction with little resources to facilitate their healing. Racism in the workplace or redlining of certain neighborhoods. Are there LGBTQ persons who feel shunned or disconnected? Are farmers faced with a bad crop due to climate and soil issues? How might we cultivate little pockets of compassion in the gaps between the fullness of God's kingdom and our present reality?

Where are places we can experience a mutuality of love, tending to the "unity that we already are"?

Community—Seeking togetherness

As we listen, as we love, as we make connections and spend time together, we will often find we are building community together. Time is the fertilizer of good relationships. Being intentional about being together in a regular rhythm and being focused and present is foundational to the community-building stage.

We try to be story collectors. Remembering the names of each person we meet. Asking questions about where our conversation left off. How did the job interview go? I know the breakup was tough, how are you doing with that? I know you said your boss was a jerk, we've been praying alongside you, any changes there? The listening and loving don't stop like we are checking off the boxes to bait and switch someone into becoming a Christian.

The movements of the loving first journey are not a causal logic process. It's not, let's do steps one, two, three, to get to _____ result. Each movement of the journey is innately good in its own right. God wants us to listen well. God wants us to love people in our communities. God wants us to build relationships together slowly over time. God wants us to share our faith in non-sketchy ways. God wants to see little healing communities spring up in every nook and cranny of life. Each movement is a set of holy habits that are intrinsically beautiful and right.

Real community doesn't typically just happen. We need to seek after it. Listening. Loving. Learning. These are key practices in cultivating community that is good, real, and whole. Often there are signs that relationships are growing deeper. We remember each other's names. We start to gel. We want to hang out more. We start a group text. We start to genuinely feel cared for and connected.

Share Jesus—Forming togetherness

This doesn't have to be as intimidating as it sounds. If we are listening and loving well, if community is starting to form, people will naturally begin to move into the spiritual. When we are sharing life together in a deep way, we just need to feel for the Holy Spirit nudges. As we listen and love, people will naturally be intrigued. They will ask questions. Then we know togetherness is starting to coalesce.

Most of the time, they will invite us to pray for them or send positive vibes. They will respond to our curiosity with curiosity. Trying to figure out what's different about us.

Sharing Jesus is not about trying to convert someone. It's about sharing our own faith story in a no pressure and organic way. I often must preface, "So you know I'm a Christian, right, but not that kind." Or more simply, "I pray because it helps me . . ." or "I find meditation really useful."

Sometimes I start with a spiritual component that some would call "secular" (personally I resist falling into that false dichotomy). I might start by reading a poem and asking people to reflect on what stood out to them. Or, "Does anyone have a poem you appreciate that you are willing to read?" I have a music playlist for states I have visited and places where I spend a lot of time. Each playlist includes musicians from that state or region. So I might say, "Hey you know this musician is from here? Can I play this song from my iPhone? Did anyone find anything spiritual in that song?"

Some communities move slower than others. Sometimes if you have done the deep relationship-building work, everyone will welcome a Jesus story and a couple questions. Other times we do the Jesus story as an add-on. We encourage people to show up early or stay late next week. We explain what we plan to do.

We also share this work so it's not one person tasked with doing the spiritual stuff every week. We ask who would like to lead the prayer next time. Who would be willing to share a Jesus story. This gives participants in the community growth opportunities. It's one thing to bow in prayer, it's another to lead it. It's one thing to participate in a Jesus story, it's another to share one.

Here also is the place where we explore ancient spiritual practices like contemplative prayer. Everyone in the group doesn't need to identify as a "Christian" in order to enjoy these practices. The practices themselves help us all turn to solitude, to make the journey from the false and illusory self towards the true self. We trust the Holy Spirit to meet each person in an appropriate way to them.

Church—Deepening togetherness

Now once we have formed deep relationships, and introduced these explicitly spiritual elements, we are starting to see a compassionate, real, and whole community start to spring up. People are committed to the group in a different way. Apprenticeship relationships are starting to form. We are connecting in between gatherings.

People have started to get real, sharing struggles and blockers to spiritual growth. We might want to formally create a rule of life, with key values and agreed-upon practices and rhythms. We continue to share leadership of the different aspects of the group. Each person can be invited to play a role.

At some point we might introduce the sacraments of baptism and the Lord's Supper. Communion often becomes a normal part of these gatherings. People will ask about contributing to the group, articulating a desire to give back. When we begin to take a formal offering, it is often best if the group decides together where the donations will go.

The key marker of where church has started to form is that we are intentionally connecting with and worshiping

God in some way. There is an upward movement of deepening connection.

I often think of the four marks of the Nicene Creed as a good framework for when a church community has formed. The community is *one*, *holy*, *catholic*, and *apostolic*. Those four words really describe four interlocking relationships. One, the inward relationship of community and belonging. Holy, the upward relationship of being transfigured in our interaction with God. Catholic, an ofward relationship with the wider church across time and space. Apostolic, an outward relationship with those who are not connected with any church.

It's important to consider the minimal ecclesiology of Jesus here: "Where two or three gather in my name, there am I with them" (Matthew 18:20). Where there are people gathered around the Risen Jesus, there is the church.

Repeat—Multiplying togetherness

Repeat is simply about multiplying togetherness. Denise has been coming to Burritos and Bibles, but now she wants to start Church 3.1. Our group has outgrown the space, so we need to think about a second site. People are asking for more time together, so we add another night. Lots of young families are showing up to our dinner church (a community meal with a Jesus story), and they want to stay later and do something together. So we start Eat. Pray. Play., an expression specifically for these young families where we eat, do arts and crafts, swap stories, and pray out.

There are endless possibilities, but the key is we are always thinking about starting the process over. How are we continuing to listen, love, build community, and where is the Spirit taking us next.

Whole together

In *Together*, US Surgeon General Vivek Murthy tells the story of coming to the realization that underlying many of the medical conditions he was treating every day was what so many of his patients described as their feeling of a "lack of belonging."[8] The sense of isolation that is so pervasive in the modern world was leading to increases in the state of loneliness. Loneliness, like a toxic cycle, affected other aspects of physical and mental well-being.

Murthy writes, "Building a more connected world holds the key to solving these and many more of the personal and societal problems confronting us today."[9] From the middle of the pandemic, he offered helpful and practical suggestions on how to increase human connection that heals our isolation and loneliness. His suggestions very much synergize with the Fresh Expressions way of being church and so I want to put them in conversation here.

Murthy suggested four key strategies to help us navigate crises and heal our social world for generations into the future:

1. Spend time each day with those you love. Murthy suggests this is not simply people who live in your household, but also other members of your lifeline. If they are physically distanced, utilize videoconference to hear their voices and see their faces. Devote at least fifteen minutes each day to connecting with those you care about.
2. Focus on each other. We should seek to eliminate distractions while interacting with others. Don't try to multitask. Try to give the other person the gift of full attention and genuinely listen.

3. Embrace solitude. Murthy believes the first step towards building stronger connections with others is to build a stronger connection with oneself. Solitude gives us space to be with our own feelings and thoughts, to explore our creativity, to connect with nature. Prayer, meditation, art, music, time outdoors, can all be sources of solitary comfort and joy.

4. Help and be helped. Service is a form of human connection that reminds us of our value and purpose in life. Both giving and receiving strengthen our social bonds. Check on a neighbor, seek advice, smile at a stranger; these kinds of small acts can strengthen our social bonds.[10]

Fresh Expressions of Church are one practical way to embody these practical suggestions. We simply find a friend or family member (or several), in some area of our life. We prayerfully discover a simple way to love the people in our relational network. We deepen relationships with them in an intentional way. We share our faith in Jesus when opportunities present themselves. We encourage those coming to faith to form a small Christian community where they are and connect them to the wider church.

I often encourage people to think of cultivating these communities in the same way we think about organizing our family life. Think of the basic tasks many of us do every day in a family. Someone must start the coffee pot, let the pets out or walk them. We get the kids up, dressed, and ready for school. We purchase groceries to keep in the fridge and pantry. We prepare meals to share. We check in on one another. We help with homework. We get people where they need to be. The love within a family doesn't just happen, it must be organized.

Sometimes within families we organize special occasions. We plan a birthday party or a wedding. We decorate for a holiday. We organize all the details of a family vacation. We create the environment for community to happen, and then there are the relational aspects of what happens in those spaces. We have conversations. We exchange touch. We connect others to each other. We laugh at jokes. We share food.

These are familiar skills that many of us have been using our entire lives. Community doesn't just happen . . . it must be organized. But it's very practical. Why then when we think of "church planting" or "evangelism" do we default to some really difficult ideas about scouring a community, looking for people we can invite to a worship service in a church building? As we have seen, this is not the way Jesus taught the disciples to be the church. If we have made evangelism and church planting so difficult that any follower of Jesus can't do it, we are doing something unfaithful to the design of Jesus.

Starting good, real, and whole expressions of church is a form of "organized love." Just as we organize love for our friends and family in small practical ways, we do that to cultivate small faith communities that disrupt the isolation and heal our loneliness.

Fresh Expressions are a way to spend time each day with those you love, while inviting others to experience that community with us. They give us environments to pause and focus on each other. Where we can really listen, eliminate distractions, and try to give the other person the gift of full attention. Part of our spiritual rhythm is to embrace solitude through basic spiritual practices like prayer, meditation, art, music, and time outdoors. These communities provide a place to help and be helped. As we hone our compassion instinct, the thread of our innate goodness that traces back to the garden where our story began, we find the union we already are.

These sacred circles of connection often happen around common activities and give us a way to be around others and relieve feelings of loneliness. Within the community we can encourage one another towards healthy habits like maintaining a balanced diet and regular exercise to prevent the physical effects of loneliness. We can also hold each other accountable about our sleep patterns. Improving sleep quality reduces fatigue and feelings of disconnection. We can check in about our online habits: have they become harmful and addictive?

These communities can be places of holistic healing, but that doesn't mean we discourage consultation with professionals. If we or someone in our community is battling depression or anxiety, we should find a good doctor or a therapist who can help. Thinking holistically includes leaning on science, research, and medications to live healthier and more joyful lives. We often overemphasize one dimension of our well-being at the exclusion of others. Physical, emotional, and social well-being are equally important. However, it is often the social dimension that is neglected the most.

As Dr. Murthy reminds us, "What often matters is not the quantity or frequency of social contact but the quality of our connections and how we feel about them."[11] Faith communities should be a place where we cultivate quality relationships. Quantity is secondary.

Yet for much of history churches have been focused on creating a quantity of relationships rather than quality of relationships. How many people, how much they give: This is the sign of a "successful" community. This is peculiar when it comes to our commitment to follow a Messiah who invested heavily in a small group of people for three years. A rabbi who taught about the value of small things, like mustard seeds, and how one small act of kindness like giving a cup of cold water to a little one can have tremendous holistic impact, in this life and the next.

If we are going to help heal our society of loneliness, we each need to celebrate the beauty of the small again. Learning to highlight the profound beauty of one person growing spiritually. One small community where people genuinely care for one another. One little space that was once a stronghold of isolation and is now a bastion of togetherness. Awakening one person to the goodness they already are.

Small whole communities. Enough of them. Can heal the whole world.

An Adventure between the Gardens

See, the home of God is among mortals.
He will dwell with them;
they will be his peoples,
and God himself will be with them and be their God;
he will wipe every tear from their eyes.
Death will be no more;
mourning and crying and pain will be no more,
for the first things have passed away.
—REVELATION 21:3–4 NRSVue

Life is an adventure between the gardens.
Life begins in a garden, starts again in a garden, and continues on eternally in a garden.

We began in that first garden in a kind of cosmic playground where humanity walks with God in the cool of the day. God invites human beings, made in the image of God, to care for the garden, to be stewards of its wonders. God shares power with humanity, inviting us to name all the animals (Genesis 2). There is no pain there, no need, no fragmentation. The *original goodness.*

There is only one restriction, eat of this one tree and you will surely die (Genesis 3). Humanity does in fact eat of that one tree, and as promised death, separation, and loneliness enter into the picture. The goodness and unity that we already are becomes wounded, the *original trauma*. However, God's response to this new scenario is a gentle and graceful call, "Where are you?" (Genesis 3).

The second garden is a graveyard (John 19:38–42). It's a place of beauty, flowers, vines, insects, and other common garden residents, but it's also a place of death. There just beneath the surface of the beauty is a grave. In a new tomb, a body lies decaying, going through all the natural processes of rigor mortis. But suddenly and supernaturally, the body buried there begins to reverse the decay. Jesus of Nazareth is raised up, the wounds of his crucifixion and suffering still evident on his once-dead-now-risen-body (John 20).

Indeed, to eat of the fruit of the tree, surely death did come, and we tasted for the first time what it's like to be alone. But now Jesus has taken that death in himself. The empty tomb he leaves behind is a portal, an entryway to the final garden.

The final garden is familiar. It evokes a sense of déjà vu. We have been here before. There is the tree that we once knew (Revelation 22). The tree we lost access to long ago. Now we are back at the tree, but the garden is also an urban garden, a heavenly city. Once again, we can walk with God in the cool of the day, living in perfect relational harmony with God, each other, and a restored cosmos. The *original unity*.

For Christians our journey between the gardens is one of going back to the future. Our eternal destination is a restored space of our deepest past . . . "Then the angel showed me the river of the water of life, bright as crystal, flowing from the throne of God and of the Lamb through the middle of the street of the city. On either side of the river is the tree of life with its twelve kinds of fruit, producing its fruit each month, and the leaves of the tree are for the healing of the nations" (Revelation 22:1–2 NRSVue).

In between those gardens, the God who calls out "Where are you?" has been calling out over us our entire lives. God is there seeking to restore that which was broken. To heal the wounds of our *original trauma*.

That is until, in the fullness of time, the "Where are you?" God puts on flesh to get to us. God becomes Immanuel, "God *with* us" (Matthew 1:23), just as the prophets said he would (Isaiah 61). Wherever Jesus goes he creates a little Edenic environment. He leaves in his wake healed people, good people, whole people, restored communities. In Jesus, the final garden of the future is breaking into the world now.

The empty tomb, the portal to eternal life, is taken up and embodied by this community called the church. The church, a people that continue the life of Jesus in the world, also become little garden spaces dotting the landscape of empires and history. In these little pockets of Jesus' life, people find freedom, healing, and new life. There we are being shaped and re-formed for life in that final garden. We are joining the original unity now.

The final garden is a "revelation," an "unveiling" of our coming-soon future. The book of Revelation gives us a crystal-clear vision of what's coming. God doesn't leave us in the dark about this.

It's easy to look across history and notice the trajectory toward this new creation has been a bumpy ride. Unfortunately, Revelation indicates it will likely get worse before it gets better. Plagues, wars, natural disasters, and supernatural forces unleashing havoc, just to name a few of the coming hiccups. Followers of Jesus are called to be "faithful, even to the point of death" (Revelation 2:10) amid these realities, until Jesus returns triumphantly (Revelation 1:7).

We can clearly see that there are gaps between what that future looks like and our communities now. How can we discern our responsibility in this unfolding new creation? Consider some of the key features of the final garden from Revelation 21–22. There we see healing manifests both physically and relationally:

Physical. The good universe that God created as the context of love is healed:

- Our final destination is an integration of all our human technologies—a city—as well as a restored garden, and a renewed cosmos stripped free of the curse of death. Our future is a blended ecology. Somehow our greatest creations, made with sin-broken materials, will be redeemed. (Revelation 21:2)
- Any physical needs we may experience will be met by Jesus. The bubbling well of eternal life Jesus gives us in this life becomes a river in the new creation. (Revelation 21:6)
- The ultimate image of accessibility. Gates are always open, and there is no threat of attack. (Revelation 21:25)
- The river of life has been fully restored, flowing from the new temple, which is now the person of God. (Revelation 22:1–2)
- Our future is in our past. We are back at the tree of life. We once again have access to the tree. This is a restored Eden, a garden-city. (Revelation 22:2)

- The tree bears different kinds of fruit, providing sustenance year-round. Good news: we will still eat in the new creation! Bad news (for carnivores): we will all be fruitarians. (Revelation 22:2)
- God is the holy of holies, and the entire universe has become the temple. The ultimate image of original unity. (Revelation 21:22) Creation will be the same but remarkably different. The fully embodied presence of God will illuminate the cosmos. (Revelation 22:5)

Relational. Human beings created for loving relationship are healed:

- God will be present in a way that we have never experienced. God's presence is healing. Our tears, the memory of what was, will be with us, but God will tenderly wipe away all suffering from our face. (Revelation 21:3–4)
- Jesus has taken his rightful place on the throne; his Lordship is fully realized. (Revelation 21:5)
- Tribal identities will have continuity, but all people have been reunified as one new humanity. The healing sparked at Pentecost is fully realized. We are made whole. Those who governed peoples will submit to the rightful Lordship of Jesus. (Revelation 21:24)
- Whatever differences we had among the nations will be settled. We will be healed of the collective wounds of war, poverty, slavery, and discrimination. We will live together around a healing tree. (Revelation 22:2)
- Worship will be a prominent feature of this new life. We will be fully restored as "image bearers of God." We will represent him in our original goodness and glory. (Revelation 22:4)

What if we were to choose just some of these features and ask what that might look like in our families, workplaces, congregations, and larger communities?

Jesus announced, once, to his disciples, "For where two or three are gathered in my name, I am there among them" (Matthew 18:20 NRSVue). Where people are gathering around the Risen Jesus as a community of love and forgiveness, *there* is the church.

The aim of the Christian life is the embodiment of Christ's presence. This reality begins in our lives *now* . . . "Therefore, if anyone is in Christ, the new creation has come: The old has gone, the new is here!" (2 Corinthians 5:17).

We become qualitatively different persons who embody the future hope of new creation in the present. As we do this together, we can manifest elements of the new creation in our communities both physically and relationally. What if we were to choose just some of these features and seek to embody them with our lives? For instance:

Physical

- We can integrate our cities with green technologies, and build in sustainability from the beginning. We can repurpose church facilities for this work.
- We can be involved in creation care, or stewardship of God's "very good" earth. The decisions we make over the next ten years will determine the kind of world our children inhabit. A planet that is sick and decaying or thriving and alive is our choice now. We can make decisions today with the next seven generations in mind.
- We can emphasize the Lordship of Jesus in a climate of political extremism. We can call for divisive parties

to submit their agendas and mutually work for the betterment of all people.

- We can meet the physical needs of those experiencing poverty, food insecurity, or homelessness.
- We can re-envision the "parish" in a way that church is not just limited to a facility owned by us, but the community itself is a temple. We can help Christian communities spring up in every space where people do life.
- In an age in which "church" has become inaccessible for most people, we can reimagine a church of unending accessibility. Church that is available right where we live, 24/7, that speaks a contextual language we can understand.
- We can change our diets and consumption habits so that we do not damage the world so prolifically. We can grow community gardens, and help people learn how to eat better.

Relational

- We can cultivate Christian communities that become places of healing rather than harm. Places where real grief can be expressed, and comfort offered, as we seek to restore people to physical, emotional, and spiritual health.
- We can honor people's racial and cultural differences, while also finding common ground. We can move beyond inculturation, toward interinculturation, in which people of different perspectives, cultures, and even religions can exchange truth. Moving toward the unity that we already are.

- We can reimaigine our community as a place known to be a healing tree. Where people are safe to bear their real wounds in an ecosystem of grace.
- Amid the realities of racism, oppression, and inequality, we can work to have our community resemble the great diverse multitude gathered around the tree of life.
- We can lay aside exceptionalism and be healed of the collective wounds of war, poverty, slavery, and discrimination.
- We can make worship a part of our every breath, rather than a service that we attend on Sundays.

Obviously, the church, the "body of Christ," is an essential part of this scenario. Jesus founded and is forming the church as his ongoing incarnation in the world. The church can be a key instrument of this new creation work.

Thus, the adventure of living between the gardens is about cultivating little new creation gardens. The most essential thing we can do is cultivate communities that form people who live in loving union with Jesus. Persons indwelled by Christ, who live, love, think, and act like Jesus. The goal of Christian spirituality is union with Christ that results in Christlike character and is shared with others. Churches are communities of people who embody the life of Jesus in the world.

These little communities become future colonies of God's final garden, spreading subversively all over the fallen empires of the world. They are communities where we make the journey through the three movements, *good*, *alone*, *together*. They are communities of gift than can heal a lonely world. Every one of us has a part to play in making that new creation real. Right now.

Is there one small thing you could do to start today? This isn't about adding one more thing to your full life. Think about the things you already do, in the places you already do them. Do you have a friend or several who will gather with you to start one small community? What you create together could save a life.

Just remember, you are *never alone*. There is one calling from the depths of your soul saying, "I am with you always, till the end of the age."

Acknowledgments

This book about community is the product of a community. I'm grateful to the great cloud of witnesses who loved me into being.

Jill Beck, my partner in life and ministry—you are my person.

For my first and favorite community—Emily, Ariel, Kaitlin, Caitlin Jean, Donald, Melly, Alexander, and Angel—thanks for letting me be your dad, and pop pop to your babies.

McKinley. I will not forget you, little bro. Your death is bringing life to others every day. I'll see you at the block party soon. Hold me a seat.

To the St Markans in Ocala, Florida. We have lived this journey together. Not many congregations would decide to turn their space into a sober housing program for men experiencing homelessness. But you did that. Thanks for rallying around an orphan infant in the waters of my baptism and making good on your promise to raise me in a community of love and forgiveness. And thanks for letting me come home to serve. Ms. Shirley Harville, much love for putting up with the little rascal messing up your keys as you played the organ, and thanks for letting me do that again today as your pastor.

To all of you who partnered together with us in the cultivation of these little healing communities in every nook and cranny of life, you are my heroes. You have brought healing where there was harm, light where there was darkness, hope where there was despair, and togetherness where there was isolation.

For all those who have mentored me over the years, there are too many of you to name. However, I am particularly grateful to Elaine Heath for shaping my thinking in this space, for reviewing the manuscript, and for providing the foreword. For Michael Moynagh, my spiritual father across the pond. You taught me that the church is a gift that can heal a lonely world.

Thanks to the Herald Press team, especially Amy Gingerich, Laura Leonard Clemens, Sara Versluis, and editors extraordinaire Elisabeth Ivey and Margot Starbuck. My name might be on the cover, but this was a community effort. We made *Never Alone* together.

To my students. I have learned more than I have taught. You give me hope for the church and the world.

And finally, to my colleagues and collaborators in good trouble at the University of Florida Department of Sociology . . . Go Gators.

Notes

INTRODUCTION

1. Vivek Murthy, *The U.S. Surgeon General's Advisory on Firearm Violence: A Public Health Crisis in America*, 2024, https://www.hhs.gov/sites/default/files/firearm-violence-advisory.pdf.

2. Vivek Murthy, Office of the Surgeon General (OSG), *Our Epidemic of Loneliness and Isolation: The U.S. Surgeon General's Advisory on the Healing Effects of Social Connection and Community* (Washington, DC: US Department of Health and Human Services, 2023), PMID: 37792968.

3. Manuel Castells, *The Rise of the Network Society* (Oxford and Malden, MA: Blackwell, 2000), xvii–xviii.

4. Jonathan Haidt, *The Anxious Generation: How the Great Rewiring of Childhood Is Causing an Epidemic of Mental Illness* (London: Allen Lane, 2024).

5. Haidt, 22–23.

6. Robert D. Putnam, *Bowling Alone: The Collapse and Revival of American Community*, rev. and updated (New York: Simon & Schuster, 2020).

7. Howard Thurman, *Jesus and the Disinherited* (Boston: Beacon Press, 2022), 11.

8. Vivek Murthy, *Our Epidemic of Loneliness and Isolation*, 16.

9. Darren M. Slade, Adrianna Smell, Elizabeth Wilson, and Rebekah Drumsta, "Percentage of U.S. Adults Suffering from Religious Trauma: A Sociological Study," *SHERM* 5, no. 1, Global Center for Religious Research (Summer 2023): 1–28.

10. Vivek Hallegere Murthy, *Together: The Healing Power of Human Connection in a Sometimes Lonely World* (New York: Harper Wave, 2020).

11. Michael Moynagh and Michael Adam Beck, *The 21st Century Christian: Following Jesus Where Life Happens* (Oviedo, FL: Higher Life Publishing, 2021). Michael Moynagh, *Giving the Church: The Christian Community through the Looking Glass of Generosity* (London: SCM Press, 2024).

12. Walter Brueggeman, *Praying the Psalms: Engaging Scripture and the Life of the Spirit*, 2nd ed. (Eugene, OR: Cascade Books, 2007), 2–3.

13. Henri J M. Nouwen, *Encounters with Merton* (Crossroad Publishing, 2017), 16.

14. Thomas Merton, *New Seeds of Contemplation* (New York: New Directions Books, 1961), 40.

15. Victor W. Turner, *The Ritual Process: Structure and Anti-structure* (Ithaca, NY: Cornell University Press, 1977), 94–95.

CHAPTER 1

1. Ran Jackson, Cory Asbury, and Caleb Culver, "Reckless Love," track 1 on *Reckless Love* (Bethel Music, 2018).
2. Thomas Merton, *New Seeds of Contemplation*. (New York: New Directions Books, 1961), 48.
3. Merton, *New Seeds*, 40.
4. Dacher Keltner, *Born to Be Good: The Science of a Meaningful Life* (New York, W. W. Norton & Company, 2009), 181.
5. Keltner, *Born to Be Good*, 51.
6. Paul Ekman, "Darwin's Compassionate View of Human Nature," *Journal of the American Medical Association* 303/6 (10 Febuary 2010), 557–58.
7. Paul Ekman, *Emotions Revealed: Recognizing Faces and Feelings to Improve Communication and Emotional Life* (New York: Henry Holt, 2003).
8. Jennifer Mascaro and Charles Raison, "The Body of Compassion" in P. Gilbert, ed., *Compassion: Concepts, Research and Applications*, 1st ed. (Milton Park, UK: Routledge, 2017), 89.
9. Penny Spikins, "Prehistoric Origins: The Compassion of Far Distant Strangers" in P. Gilbert, ed. *Compassion*, 18–19.
10. Spikins, 28.
11. Aristotle, *Politics*, 1.1253a, Aristotle in 23 Volumes, Vol. 21, H. Rackham, trans. (Cambridge, MA: Harvard University Press; London: William Heinemann Ltd., 1944).
12. Eddie Harmon-Jones and Michael Inzlicht, eds., *Social Neuroscience: Biological Approaches to Social Psychology. Frontiers of Social Psychology* (New York: Routledge, Taylor & Francis Group, 2016), 2.
13. e.g., Brothers, 1997; Gazzaniga, 1985, in Harmon-Jones and Inzlicht, 3.
14. e.g., Cacioppo and Bernston, 1992; Klein and Kihlstrom, 1998, in Harmon-Jones and Inzlicht, 3.
15. e.g., Adolphs, 1999, 2003; Blascovich, 2000; Ochsner and Lieberman, 2001; Winkielman, Bernston, and Cacioppo, 2001, in Harmon-Jones and Inzlicht, 3.
16. Mesulam and Perry, 1972, in Harmon-Jones and Inzlicht, 2.
17. Harmon-Jones and Inzlicht, 4.

CHAPTER 2

1. Michael Fishbane, italics his, quoted in T. Desmond Alexander and David W. Baker, eds. *Dictionary of the Old Testament: Pentateuch* (Downers Grove, IL: InterVarsity Press, 2003), 23.
2. Sherry Turkle, *Alone Together: Why We Expect More from Technology and Less from Each Other* (New York: Basic Books, 2017), 238.
3. Vivek Hallegere Murthy, *Together: The Healing Power of Human Connection in a Sometimes Lonely World* (New York: Harper Wave, 2020), 24.
4. Murthy, *Together*, 21.
5. Murthy, *Together*, 23.
6. Thomas Merton, *New Seeds of Contemplation* (New York: New Directions Books, 1961), 40.
7. Merton, *New Seeds*, 30.
8. Merton, *New Seeds*, 47.

9. Jean Case et al., *Calculating Torture: Analysis of Federal, State, and Local Data Showing More Than 122,000 People in Solitary Confinement in U.S. Prisons and Jails* (Solitary Watch and Unlock the Box, 2023), https://solitarywatch.org/wp-content/uploads/2023/05/Calculating-Torture-Report-May-2023-R2.pdf.

10. Merton, *New Seeds*, 53.

CHAPTER 3

1. Robin Williams Jr., *American Society: A Sociological Interpretation*, 2nd ed. (New York: Knopf, 1965).

2. Vivek Hallegere Murthy, *Together: The Healing Power of Human Connection in a Sometimes Lonely World* (New York: Harper Wave, 2020), 13.

3. Pierre Bourdieu, *Pascalian Meditations* (Cambridge, UK: Polity Press, 2000), 150.

4. Alan Kreider, *The Patient Ferment of the Early Church: The Improbable Rise of Christianity in the Roman Empire* (Grand Rapids, MI: Baker Academic, 2016), 39–41.

5. Kreider, 135.

CHAPTER 4

1. G. W. Allport and M. J. Ross, "Personal Religious Orientation and Prejudice," *Journal of Personality and Social Psychology* 5 (1967): 432–43.

2. Allport and Ross, 434.

3. Monika Ardelt (2003) "Empirical Assessment of a Three-Dimensional Wisdom Scale," *Research on Aging* 25, no. 3, 275–324.

4. Monika Ardelt and Cynthia S. Koenig, "Differential Roles of Religious Orientation on Subjective Well-Being and Death Attitudes in Old Age: Mediation of Spiritual Activities and Purpose in Life," in Amy L. Ai and Monika Ardelt, *Role of Faith in the Well-Being of Older Adults: Linking Theories with Evidence in an Interdisciplinary Inquiry* (Nova Science Publishers, Incorporated, 2009).

5. Ardelt and Koenig, 86.

6. S. You and S. A. Lim, "Religious Orientation and Subjective Well-being: The Mediating Role of Meaning in Life," *Journal of Psychology and Theology* 47, no. 1 (2019): 34–47; Koenig, George, and Peterson, 1998; Falkenhain and Handal, 2003; Thorson and Powell, 2000.

7. Ardelt and Koenig, 104.

8. Ardelt and Koenig, 104.

9. Ardelt and Koenig, 106.

10. Regular church attendance does not positively correlate with increased social compassion in church attenders. See the following. G. Lenski, *The Religious Factor* (Garden City, NY: Doubleday, 1963); Gordon W. Allport and J. M. Ross, "Personal Religious Orientations and Prejudice," *Journal of Personality and Social Psychology* 5 (1967): 432–33; C. Y. Glock and R. Stark, *Religion and Society in Tension* (San Francisco: Rand McNally, 1965); Milton Rokeach, "Value Systems in Religion," *Review of Religious Research* 11 (1969): 3–23; Milton Rokeach, "Religious Values and Social Compassion," *Review of Religious Research* 11 (1969): 24–39; Milton Rokeach, *The Nature of Human Values* (New York: The Free Press: 1973); James A. Christenson, "Religious Involvement, Values and Social Compassion," *Sociological Analysis* 37, no. 3 (1976): 218–27.

11. Kristin Neff, *Self-Compassion: The Proven Power of Being Kind to Yourself*, 1st ed. (New York: William Morrow, 2011), 39.

12. Listen to Tracy share her story here: "Doing Justice Together: Tracy's Story," Fresh Expressions, https://my.amplifymedia.com/freshexpressions/series/freshexparch/84623-doing-justice-together-stories/84626-stories/155879-doing-justice-together-tracys-story.

13. Thomas Merton, *New Seeds of Contemplation* (New York: New Directions Books, 1961), 51.

14. Dacher Keltner, Jason Marsh, and Jeremy Adam Smith, eds., *The Compassionate Instinct: The Science of Human Goodness*, 1st ed. (New York: W.W. Norton & Co, 2010), 35.

15. Philippe Goldin and Hooria Jazaieri, "The Compassion Cultivation Training (CCT) Program," chap. 18 in *The Oxford Handbook of Compassion Science*, ed. Emma M. Seppälä et al. (Oxford University Press, 2017), 10.1093/oxfordhb/9780190464684.013.18.

16. Merton, *New Seeds*, 42.

17. Keltner et al., *Compassionate Instinct*, 35.

CHAPTER 5

1. *Someone to Love* (1987 film), words added by Welles to Henry Jaglom's script.

2. Thomas Merton, *Conjectures of a Guilty Bystander* (New York: Doubleday: 1968), 156–58.

3. Thomas Merton, "Address to International Summit of Monks, Calcutta, India (October 19–27, 1968)," in *The Asian Journals of Thomas Merton* (New Directions: 1975), 51.

4. Thomas Merton, *New Seeds of Contemplation*. (New York: New Directions Books, 1961), 24–26.

5. Merton, *New Seeds*, 30.

6. Merton, *New Seeds*, 44.

7. Merton, *New Seeds*, 157.

8. Merton, *New Seeds*, 47.

9. Merton, *New Seeds*, 40.

10. Merton, *New Seeds*, 40.

11. Merton, *New Seeds*, 52.

12. John Wesley, *Hymns and Sacred Poems* (1739), preface, viii.

13. Manuel Castells, *The Rise of the Network Society* (Oxford and Malden, MA: Blackwell, 2000), xvii–xviii.

14. Castells, xxxi.

15. Castells, xxxi.

16. Timothy W. Luke, "Cyberspace as Meta-Nation: The Net Effects of Online E-Publicanism," *Alternatives: Global, Local, Political* 26, no. 2 (2001), 113.

17. Castells, xxix.

18. Sherry Turkle, *Alone Together: Why We Expect More from Technology and Less from Each Other* (New York: Basic Books, 2017), 238.

19. Turkle, 239.

20. Turkle, 3.

21. Michael Adam Beck and Rosario Picardo, *Fresh Expressions in a Digital Age: How the Church Can Prepare for a Post Pandemic World* (Nashville: Abingdon, 2021).

22. Jonathan Haidt, *The Anxious Generation: How the Great Rewiring of Childhood Is Causing an Epidemic of Mental Illness* (London: Allen Lane, 2024), 16.

23. Haidt, 16.

24. Haidt, 17.

25. S. Konrath, A. J. Martingano, M. Davis, and F. Breithaupt, "Empathy Trends in American Youth Between 1979 and 2018: An Update," *Social Psychological and Personality Science* (December 28, 2023) 0(0), https://doi.org/10.1177/19485506231218360; J. M. Twenge, W. K. Campbell, and E. C. Freeman, "Generational Differences in Young Adults' Life Goals, Concern for Others, and Civic Orientation, 1966–2009," *Journal of Personality and Social Psychology* 102, no. 5 (May 2012): 1045–62.

26. Michael Adam Beck, *Painting with Ashes: When Your Weakness Becomes Your Superpower* (Plano, TX: Invite, 2022).

27. Monika Ardelt and Bhavna Sharma, "Linking Wise Organizations to Wise Leadership, Job Satisfaction, and Well-Being," *Frontiers in Communication* 6 (November 2021), https://doi.org/10.3389/fcomm.2021.685850.

28. Arbinger Institute, *The Anatomy of Peace: Resolving the Heart of Conflict*, 4th ed. (Oakland, CA: Berrett-Koehler, 2022).

29. Makungu M. Akinyela, "Testimony of Hope: African Centered Praxis for Therapeutic Ends," *Journal of Systemic Therapies* 24, no. 1 (2005): 5–18, https://www.academia.edu/2324704/Testimony_of_hope_African_centered_praxis_for_therapeutic_ends.

CHAPTER 6

1. Kayanesenh Paul Williams, *Kayanerenkó:Wa: The Great Law of Peace* (Winnipeg, MB: University of Manitoba Press, 2018), 16.

2. Springtide Research, *The State of Religion and Young People 2021: Navigating Uncertainty* (Springtide Research Institute, 2021).

3. Springtide Research, *The State of Religion and Young People, 2023: Exploring the Sacred* (Springtide Research Institute, 2023).

4. Learn more about Ka:ll at KallCommunity.org.

5. See Patricia Peña, Fresh Expressions: A Bridge of Connection and Transformation in Community," Fresh Expressions," March 19, 2024, https://www.umcdiscipleship.org/articles/fresh-expressions-a-bridge-of-connection-and-transformation-in-community.

6. Learn more at EncounterTheWell.org.

7. Graham Cray, *Mission-Shaped Church: Church Planting and Fresh Expressions in a Changing Context* (New York: Seabury Books, 2010), 100.

8. Vivek Hallegere Murthy, *Together: The Healing Power of Human Connection in a Sometimes Lonely World* (New York: Harper Wave, 2020), 13.

9. Murthy, *Together*, 14.

10. Murthy, *Together*, 9.

11. Murthy, *Together*, 22.

The Author

Michael Adam Beck is the director of the Fresh Expressions House of Studies at United Theological Seminary, director of Fresh Expressions Florida, and director of Fresh Expressions for the United Methodist Church. He serves as the co-pastor of Wildwood UMC, St. Marks UMC, and Compassion UMC with his wife Jill, where 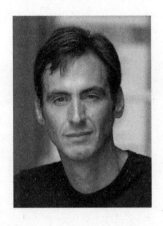 they direct addiction recovery programs, a jail ministry, a food pantry, and an interracial unity movement, and house a faith-based inpatient treatment center. He is the author or coauthor of over a dozen books, including *Deep Roots, Wild Branches* and *Contextual Intelligence*, with Leonard Sweet.